COVER DESIGN *Laminated bends*

FRONTISPIECE *Spiral staircase*

Ministry of Technology

W C Stevens & N Turner

Wood Bending Handbook

WOODCRAFT SUPPLY CORP.

WOBURN, MASS. 01801

Forest Products Research Laboratory

Manufactured in the United States of America

Woodcraft Supply Corporation
313 Montvale Avenue
Woburn, Massachusetts 01801
1978
ISBN 0-918036-06-2
LC # 77-94902

Preface

The purpose of this book is to meet the demand for information on the processes of wood bending as reflected in the many enquiries addressed to this Laboratory. It is a revision of the book entitled 'Solid and Laminated Wood Bending' which was published in 1948 but it contains data accumulated since that date and a description of new and improved techniques. In addition there are chapters on the construction of curved laminated structural members and on the bending of plywood.

It is largely a handbook of practice and is thus written from the practical viewpoint, with such theoretical background as suffices to explain the adoption of the various procedures. It would not be possible, and indeed the authors have not attempted, to deal with the many special variants of bending processes in commercial use. All of these rest upon the nature of the timber to be bent and upon the application of certain general principles. These are here set forth and clarified by the detailed treatment of some typical examples which will serve to give a lead to the ingenuity of the individual user for his own needs.

Thanks are due to members of the trade for permission to use photographs illustrating some of the processes, and each is acknowledged in the appropriate place.

T A Oxley, *Director*

Forest Products Research Laboratory
Princes Risborough
Aylesbury
Buckinghamshire
January 1970

Contents

Contents

Introduction

The practice of bending timber dates back to antiquity when man first learnt to make baskets from osier and shipwrights no longer contented themselves with making boats from hollowed-out logs. Since wood in its natural state has strongly marked elastic properties, a bend made from such resilient material would retain its shape only so long as it was securely held in place by adjacent members of a structure. Moreover, it would be extremely difficult, if not impossible, to bend thick pieces to a small radius of curvature; consequently curved boat stems, for example, were hewn or sawn from limbs of trees having a curvature roughly the same as that required. This method of producing curved members has very obvious limitations and is rarely practised nowadays, and in the production of various curved parts and members commonly required for the manufacture of furniture, boats, sports equipment etc., the timber is usually obtained in board or scantling form and either bandsawn or bent to shape. If the thickness of the portion to be bent is small compared with the radius of curvature, and is to be held firmly in position by adjacent structural parts when bent, wood in its natural or in its dried state may be employed.

Theoretically there is, of course, no limit to the radius of curvature or thickness of curved parts produced by band-sawing, but this method has two distinct disadvantages. In the first place, when band-sawing a curved piece of comparatively small radius of curvature it becomes necessary to saw some portion of it across the grain of the wood, with a consequent appreciable reduction in the strength of the piece as a whole. Secondly, the awkwardly shaped portions that are cut away often constitute a very serious conversion loss. Fortunately, there are means by which straight pieces of timber can be bent to shape and made to retain this shape without necessarily receiving support from adjacent members. There are two main methods of doing this: one by softening and bending the complete piece in the solid, and the other by bending and gluing together a number of thin laminations or plywood strips to produce a built-up piece of the required dimension and curvature. In commercial practice, production costs, facilities available, quality and prices of timber to be used, etc. must all be considered before deciding on the method to be adopted.

Various methods commonly employed for bending both solid and laminated wood and also plywood are described in the following pages, together with some new and improved methods of bending developed at the Laboratory. Most – though not all – the methods des-cribed have been tested at the Laboratory. It is hoped that the descriptions may prove useful to those engaged in or contemplating work of this nature, but it must be stressed that success in bending depends as much upon the skill and experience of the operators as upon any theoretical knowledge acquired from books.

The principles of wood bending

In the bending of wood or other elastic materials it is usual to assume that transverse plane sections remain plane and normal to the longitudinal fibres, i.e. end sections initially square with the faces of a piece remain square during the process of bending. From this it follows that, in the bent state, the lengths of the convex and concave faces are no longer equal as they were when originally cut. The difference in these lengths is brought about by induced compressive stresses causing the fibres on the concave face to shorten, and induced tensile stresses causing the fibres on the convex face to stretch.

Wood in its natural state exhibits elastic properties over a limited range; within this range strain is proportional to stress and, when the imposed force producing the stress is removed, the strain also disappears and the wood returns to its original state and dimension. It follows that if the limiting stress is not exceeded anywhere within the piece, a bend made from such material will spring back to its original shape when the forces producing it are removed. When this limiting stress value is exceeded however, stress is no longer proportional to strain, and, on removal of the applied force, some permanent deformation is usually observed to have taken place. Further stressing will ultimately induce strains sufficient to cause fracturing of the piece, generally apparent first on the stretched convex face. Maximum strain intensities will naturally occur on the extreme inner and outer surfaces of a bent piece and will increase as the radius of the bend decreases for any given thickness. The limiting radius is thus dependent upon the magnitude of the strains that can be induced on these faces without causing fractures.

Most timbers in their natural state cannot be bent to an appreciably small radius of curvature without either fracturing or retaining elastic properties sufficient to cause them to spring back to approximately their original shape on removal of the bending forces. But some species when subjected to heat in the presence of moisture (usually by steaming or boiling) become semi-plastic and their compressibility is very considerably increased. In this state comparatively small compressive stresses are capable of producing appreciable strains without fracturing the material. This treatment has much less effect upon the tensile properties of these woods and the limiting radius of curvature then becomes dependent on the maximum permissible tensile stress and the strain of the stretched fibres on the convex face. Even so, this limiting radius may be much smaller than before, since appreciably more shortening of the fibres near the concave face may occur before the breaking point in tension is reached than when no treatment is applied. In a bend made from untreated wood, the neutral axis, along which no change in length has occurred, coincides much more closely with a line situated midway between the convex and concave surfaces than a bend made from treated material. In the latter, there is a pronounced tendency for the neutral axis to move towards the convex surface, so that the proportion of the wood in tension is reduced and that in compression is increased (*see Fig. 1*).

A second factor of considerable importance, introduced as a result of the treatment, is the tendency of the now more plastic material to retain its shape after bending, particularly if dried under restraint. By holding such material to shape after bending, and subsequently drying and cooling it, the wood tends to become rigid and 'set' almost exactly to the curved shape imposed on it by bending.

The precise mechanism involved in the plastic deformation of stressed heat-treated wood is not fully understood, nor can it be stated with certainty why some timbers are considerably more responsive to such treatment than others. In general, most of the temperate zone hardwoods react favourably to treatment, but many of the tropical hardwoods and most of the softwoods are refractory in this respect and hence are little suited to bending in solid form. The manner in which a good bending species, such as *ash*, will react is illustrated in *Figs. 2* and *3*, which show the stress-strain relationships in tension and compression of sample specimens before and after steaming. These show clearly that the effect of the treatment is:

1 to cause the compressive strain to increase rapidly with stress above a certain value;

2 to increase very considerably the ultimate strain in compression;

3 to induce only comparatively slight changes in the tensile properties of the wood.

It has already been shown that the maximum stress and strain in tension determine the limiting radius of curvature for bending without fracture and, in practice, it will be found that the stretched convex face will tend to fracture long before the compressed concave face has been strained to the limit. Obviously, if it were possible to impose the maximum permissible compression on the concave face of a bend without, at the same time, inducing such stress on the fibres near the convex face as to strain them beyond the limit, the radius of curvature could be decreased yet further. This, in effect, is the underlying principle of the method of bending with the aid of a supporting strap.

In the normal application of this method, the stretched convex face is supported by means of a band of steel or other suitable material placed over and secured to it in such a way that the strain is limited by mechanical restraint. In its simplest form this band or strap consists of a thin steel strip fitted with wooden or steel angles or endstops that bear closely on the ends of the piece to be bent. Neglecting the stretch in the steel, and assuming the endstops fit closely initially, it follows that during the bending process, virtually no stretching of the fibres can take place and the limiting radius is dependent solely upon the ultimate strain in compression.

In actual practice a certain amount of stretch sometimes occurs, and in certain instances special adjustable endstops are fitted so as to regulate the amount, but in no case should this be allowed to exceed the breaking point. A typical failure in tension resulting from the lack of adequate support is shown in *Plate 2*, and a typical failure caused by over-compressing the inner face of a bend is illustrated in *Plate 3*. The smallest possible radius of curvature for any piece of wood is reached when both the inner and outer surfaces are on the point of fracturing.

FIG I *Effect of steaming treatment on the position of the neutral axis in a bend*

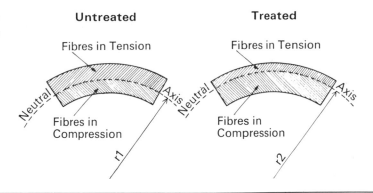

FIG 2 *Effect of steaming on the stress/strain relationship in tension of home-grown ash*

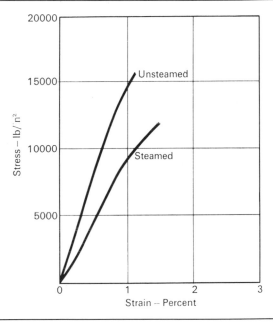

FIG 3 *Effect of steaming on the stress/strain relationship in compression of home-grown ash*

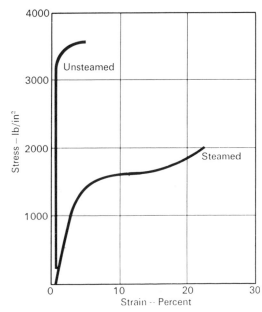

PLATE I *Examples of solid bends
used in industry*

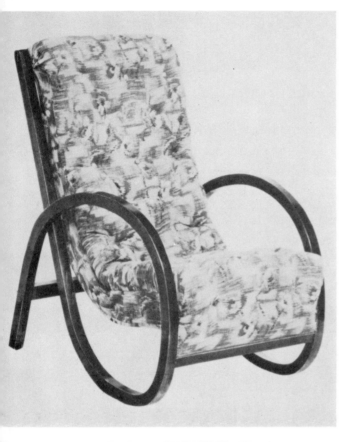

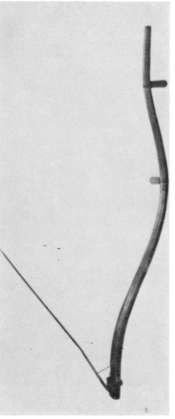

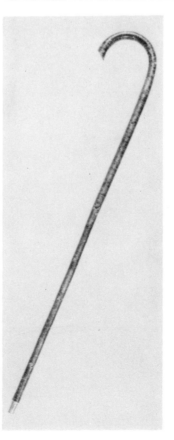

PLATE 2 *Typical failure resulting from inadequate support on the convex face of a bend*

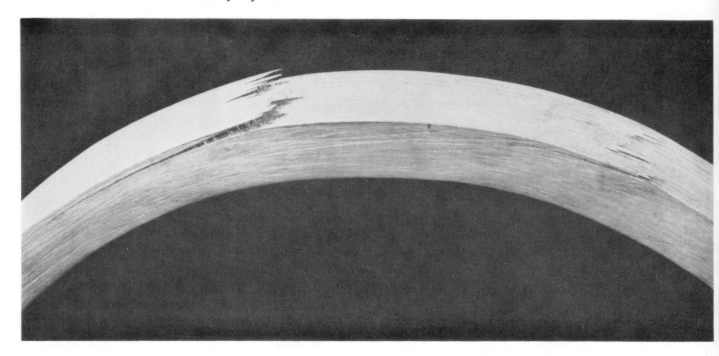

PLATE 3 *Typical failure resulting from over compressing the concave face of a bend*

Part A: Solid bending

7

B

1 *The selection and preparation of bending material*

Quality

Care in selecting wood for bending is essential for appreciable compressive strains are likely to be imposed upon the fibres and the structure generally. Planes of weakness, caused by the presence of defects such as knots, ingrown bark, surface checks, etc., will start fractures in and around these planes when comparatively little straining has occurred. The use of timber containing such defects should be avoided as far as possible to minimize losses due to failure of the wood in bending. Should it prove impossible to eliminate such defects entirely, the bending blank should be set up so that the defect is near the convex face and hence near or on the neutral axis where the imposed strains are at a minimum. Ideally, straight-grained, clear material should be specially selected for bending work, particularly if the bend is severe.

Species

In selecting a species of timber suitable for the job in hand, several factors should be taken into consideration, such as availability of material, bending properties, strength properties of the material after bending, etc. Bent furniture parts, for instance, are usually made from beech or oak since these timbers are in reasonable supply, have good bending properties and are much used for the manufacture of furniture in general. The manufacturer of sports goods, however, generally selects such species as ash or hickory for the production of hockey and lacrosse sticks, on account of their high impact strength and toughness as well as their good bending properties. Data on the bending properties of a large number of different timbers are given in *Table 1* which has been compiled from the results of tests carried out at the Forest Products Research Laboratory. It indicates a safe radius of curvature to which the timbers may be bent, so that not more than 5 per cent of the total number of bent pieces will fracture during the process. It needs to be added that the data in the table refer to good quality, air-dried material, one-inch thick and steamed at atmospheric pressure.

The influence that supporting straps have on the limiting radius of curvature is indicated very clearly in this table, and also the greatly superior bending qualities of such woods as elm, ash and beech, as compared with, say, mahogany, teak or spruce. It is of interest to note that there is not a great difference in the bending properties of ash, beech and oak despite the fact that the first named is commonly regarded as being a bending timber *par excellence*.

Ash, though undoubtedly an excellent bending wood, is unusually susceptible to the presence of pin knots near the compression face, which are very prone to produce buckling or compression failures. Moreover, if the grain runs out on the tension face there is a pronounced tendency for it to lift when the strap is finally removed. Elm, on the other hand, has exceptionally good bending qualities and it also appears generally to be remarkably tolerant of defects, though naturally, as in all woods, they have an adverse effect on its bending properties.

Trees

Once the species and quality of the timber required for a particular job has been decided, the question next arises as to what precautions should be taken to ensure that the trees selected will in fact provide the maximum quantity of material most suitable for the purpose. On this subject there are considerable differences of opinion and few bending firms seem to be entirely in agreement as to the distinguishing features that mark good quality bending timber in the round. Factors such as age, rate of growth, soil characteristics, etc., undoubtedly have a bearing on the subject, though from tests carried out at the Laboratory the indications are that provided clear, straight-grown material can be obtained, these factors are of secondary importance.

It has been considered, however, that some of the best bending ash, for instance, is to be obtained from trees which have been grown on a fertile, freely-drained loam over limestone or in the red sandstone districts. Test data would indicate however that locality of growth is not a major factor in determining bending quality. For most timbers, also, the second length above the spread of the butt provides the best material, although for many types of bends virtually any part of the tree below the crown can be used providing it is clear of defects.

Wood from near the heart is generally to be avoided and trees having an oval or elliptical cross-section with the heart much off centre are unlikely to produce satisfactory material. Such trees are likely to contain tension wood which is liable to cause severe distortion of the pieces cut for bending when these are being steamed or dried. Very old trees, or trees that have grown either very rapidly or very slowly, do not usually yield the best material.

Trees attacked by fungus of any sort are worthless for bending as the wood is liable to be brittle and may break right across the section during the bending operation.

Moisture content

The bending properties of timber are influenced by the moisture content. Most species can be bent in the green state soon after felling; some species, however, such as wych elm, sweet chestnut and oak, if bent while green to a small radius of curvature, are liable to rupture as a result of hydraulic pressures built up within the moisture laden cells. Apart from the fact that the forces required for bending are greater, it may be said that the properties of wood air-dried, or kiln-dried, to a moisture content of about 25 per cent differ little from similar material in the green state. Experience has shown, moreover, that supporting straps can be removed with impunity sooner after bending the drier material and that a shorter time is required for drying and setting to shape with reduced tendency for the bend to distort or split during this process.

The disadvantages of using air-dried material are as follows

1 fine surface checks which may have developed in seasoning and have passed unnoticed may result in compression failures;
2 the steaming treatment in wetting the dried wood may cause it to distort before bending;
3 bending by hand is more arduous.

The production of satisfactory bends from material at a moisture content of appreciably less than about 25 per cent is quite possible, especially when using a bending machine, but the risk of fracture occurring on the convex face is greater due to the considerably higher forces induced. In addition, very dry material may buckle and wrinkle on the concave face and for this reason the use of such material is not recommended. If stock is received in a state which is considered too dry for solid bending, a worthwhile improvement in the bending properties may be achieved by immersion in cold water for a short period say overnight.

Machining

Once a decision has been reached regarding the species, quality and selection of the timber, the blanks or specimens must be prepared for the softening treatment. These should all be cut exactly to length with squared ends, leaving sufficient material for nailing tie-bars if this operation is found to be necessary. Longitudinal movements may occur during the steaming process however, and it would be advisable in these instances, especially where several pieces are bent side by side in one operation,

to trim to length after steaming and immediately prior to bending. Allowances must be made for some distortion of the cross-section during bending, for subsequent shrinkage and for the inevitable deviations from the exact shape required associated with solid bending. A smooth surface on the blanks is very desirable, since ridges tend to induce buckling, and for this reason, planed timber is better than material straight from the saw. It is quite possible to bend shaped or moulded material of, say, round section, but where this is undertaken it must be remembered that the bending process always tends to flatten the surfaces in contact with the form and strap causing lateral expansion of the piece. Sectional distortion is sometimes of no consequence, or can be remedied by subsequent sanding of the bent part.

Experience has shown that plain-sawn material, cut and bent so that the annual rings are roughly parallel to the face of the form, gives results slightly better than quarter-sawn material bent with the rings normal to the face of the form, but the trouble entailed in securing this improvement would hardly be justified except, possibly, in the case of very severe types of bend.

2 Softening treatments

Steaming

In order to render timbers plastic and compressible so that they are in the best possible condition for bending, a supply of heat and moisture must be made available.

It has already been stated that wood at 25 to 30 per cent moisture content contains as much moisture as is necessary to render it compressible when heated. Most tests made at the Laboratory have failed to show any marked improvement in the bending qualities of wood by heating it to a temperature much above the boiling point of water, i.e. 100°C (212°F). Probably the commonest and most suitable method of obtaining the required conditions is to subject the timber to saturated steam at atmospheric pressure in a steam chest such as the one illustrated in *Fig. 4*. The essentials of such a steaming chamber are that sufficient steam is made available to maintain an average temperature of 100°C and that means are provided for readily introducing and removing the wood to be bent.

Racks or shelves for holding the timber need to be provided, and it must be remembered that certain timbers such as oak, if placed in contact with iron or steel, are liable to become badly stained. In order to economize in steam, the chest should be lagged and, provided the desired temperature can be maintained, even exhaust steam from an engine may be used. There would appear to be no great advantage in using steam at a higher pressure than atmospheric, as the bending properties of wood are not markedly increased at the higher pressures. The disadvantages of using higher pressure steam are that the chest must be made strong enough to withstand the internal pressure, and that before the door can be opened care must be taken to ensure that the pressure has dropped to zero, thus entailing a loss in production time. Very high

pressures have also been found to be detrimental to certain timbers and to result in serious discoloration.

Wood is in the best possible condition for bending when it has been heated right through to boiling point temperature, and, as a rough guide, three quarters of an hour per inch of thickness (1·8 minutes per mm) should suffice to effect this. No improvement in the bending properties results from prolonged steaming. The steaming process produces some, but not extensive, drying of green timber, but the average moisture content of air-dried wood at, say, 25 per cent moisture content is scarcely altered as a result of the steaming treatment. Very dry wood would undoubtedly pick up a certain amount of moisture, mainly on the surface, but for the most part the effect of steaming is to heat the wood, not to inject steam into the material as is sometimes supposed.

Other heating methods

Softening by steaming is the most usual means of making wood semi-plastic for bending but any treatment that heats the timber to about the boiling point of water without detriment to its structure or causing it to dry very appreciably will serve.

For example, in the cooperage industry at one time the staves for tight oak and other casks were softened by placing the partly shaped or 'raised' cask over a fire of wood shavings yet keeping the inside wet by sponging it with water. Again many walking-stick manufacturers used to soften the walking sticks and umbrella handles in heated wet sand or boiling water before bending them to shape and, where rattan cane was used, this was often

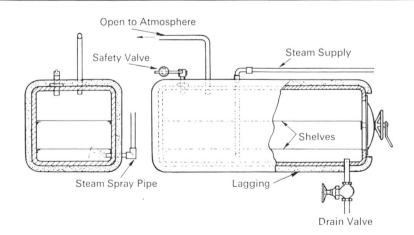

FIG 4 *Steaming chest*

Open to Atmosphere

Safety Valve

Steam Supply

Steam Spray Pipe

Lagging

Shelves

Drain Valve

softened by exposing the appropriate portions to a naked gas flame. In recent years, radio-frequency heating has been employed for softening wood that has to be bent but although this method is rapid in its application it is not much used. One reason for this apart from its expense is that non-permeable woods like oak and occasionally even in more permeable woods such as beech, there is a likelihood that the steam generated within the cells of the wood will find difficulty in escaping and will build up to a pressure sufficient to rupture the cell walls.

Chemical treatments

Various attempts have been made to render wood suitable for bending by chemical treatments but, to date, no completely satisfactory method has been discovered. One method suggested was impregnating wood with a saturated solution of urea and then heating it in an oven at a temperature of 100°C (212°F). Wood treated in this way, it was claimed, could be bent to shape either with or without a strap and it would set on cooling. Tests carried out at the Forest Products Research Laboratory showed that the bending properties of wood so treated were no different from those of wood that had been steamed. Furthermore, though it was found that drying, as well as cooling, was not essential for setting bends made in this manner, exposure of the set bends to high humidity conditions led to very rapid moisture absorption often sufficient to cause the bends to straighten out completely.

More recently a process has been developed in the United States for making wood pliable by dipping it in liquid anhydrous ammonia which boils at —33°C (—28°F). Wood suspended in this cold liquid for several minutes can be bent and twisted to any shape and hardens again as soon as the ammonia evaporates. It is stated to have proved to be satisfactory for the bending of ash, birch and elm but only in thicknesses up to $\frac{1}{8}$ inch (3·2 mm).

3 Hand bending

The term hand bending usually implies that the bending operation is performed manually even though some simple power-multiplying device, such as a lever, is employed to force the pieces to shape. Power-driven bending machinery has certain obvious advantages over the hand-operated equipment, but has also certain disadvantages and limitations. The initial cost of installing power-operated machines often proves a factor limiting their use. Furthermore, there are few universal bending machines capable of producing a really large variety of designs; indeed most complicated bends are still made by skilled hand-bending operators. Although the requisite skill can only be obtained by experience, suitable and efficient bending equipment is a great asset in such work.

The principles of bending, as already outlined, must be observed in all cases to ensure good results, but the actual methods and equipment may vary considerably. A description of all possible bending methods and types of bend would fill several volumes but it is proposed here to outline some of the methods in general use and to illustrate apparatus and equipment that has proved efficient for many of the commoner types of bend. Although the equipment illustrated here is not essential or even the most efficient for specific purposes, it is hoped that the following information, which is of a practical nature, will be a guide to those who are not thoroughly acquainted with the practice of bending in general, and will assist those who wish to modify their present technique. Many of the methods and equipment described have been tested at the Laboratory, and much of the following information is based on the experience so gained.

Bending in the cold state

The simplest type of bend is one made from untreated timber, in its natural or dried state, but with few exceptions a comparatively small radius of curvature cannot be attained with such material without fracture occurring. For most woods an approximate limit for clear straight-grained material is given by the formula $\frac{R}{S} = 50$, where R is the radius of curvature and S is the thickness of the piece. Although this formula is by no means exact, it indicates that a piece of wood one inch (25 mm) thick cannot be bent to a radius of much less than about 4 feet (1·2m) in its natural state. Such a bent piece would be extremely elastic and could not be expected to set to shape and would need to be rigidly attached to some frame-work arranged roughly to the contour of the curve desired. An example

of this type of bend may be found in the curved planking of boats which are sometimes bent in the cold state and secured in place on the frames. Where strength considerations are of little importance and only one face of a bent board is to be exposed to view, the effective thickness of the piece may be reduced and bending facilitated by removing portions from the concave face by means of saw cuts. A series of transverse parallel saw cuts or grooves may be made on what is to be the inner face of bend, which in effect reduces the thickness of the bent portion, thus reducing the limiting radius for fractureless bending and facilitating the operation generally. This method is frequently used by coffin manufacturers and by joiners in the fitting of curved risers to stairs, etc.

Hot bending (unsupported)

For bends of smaller radius that are required to retain approximately their shape, the wood needs to be heat-softened in the manner already described. Most timbers can be bent to a much smaller radius of curvature after such treatment than before, even without the aid of straps. Some idea of the reduction in the limiting radius achieved as a result of steaming may be gathered from *Table 1*, where it will be observed that for English beech, for example, the ratio of R to S is improved to a value of about 13. For making bends from steamed but unsupported material such methods as the following are usually adopted:

1 the piece may be clamped between suitably curved male and female forms as shown in *Fig. 5*;
2 the piece may be forced to shape over suitably prepared wooden, or preferably metal, forms and held in position in the manner shown in *Fig. 6*.

The first method has the disadvantage that difficulty is experienced in the drying and setting of the bent piece, and the second method is usually to be preferred.

Walking sticks made from coppice shoots of chestnut, ash and hazel may be bent after heat treatment using the latter method and the wedge or clamp may be replaced by a tie across the handle if this has been bent through an angle of 180°. A bend so tied and held can be removed from the form for quick setting. It is interesting to note that if the bark is to remain on the stick it is essential to air-dry the wood before bending, and that it is by softening and bending the wood that initial curvature and twists in the piece as cut can be removed. There are many specific applications of the method of bending steamed but unsupported timber as, for example, in the production of furniture parts and in the shipbuilding trade where planking is made from boards steamed and bent manually to shape and secured to the frames.

One other special application which needs to be dealt with here is in effect, a combination of hand and machine bending. A method frequently employed for the production of hoops for such articles as sieves, barrels, etc., and found to be very satisfactory, consists of bending a thin strip of steamed material to a diameter smaller than that actually required, by means of a hand-operated machine resembling a mangle. This machine consists essentially of two rollers which can be revolved by means of a hand wheel with a steel band of approximately 18 s.w.g. (1·2 mm) thickness attached to one of the rollers (*see Fig. 7*). After inserting one end of the steamed strip which has already been cut to length and, if necessary, scarfed at the ends, between the metal and the roller to which it is held, the machine is set in motion and the strip and band are wound on to the roller. On completion of this pre-bending operation, which should be carried out as rapidly as possible, the strip is immediately withdrawn from the machine, held by hand to prevent it uncoiling or, if necessary, recoiled and forced inside a metal hoop. The inner diameter of this hoop is equal to the outer diameter of the wooden hoop or rim required. The scarfed ends of the strip are finally joined together with small nails and the whole removed from the metal ring to accelerate the setting and drying process.

Hot bending (supported)

When the thickness of the piece and the radius of curvature are such that supporting straps are necessary to prevent fractures occurring on the stretched outer face, these straps are usually made of mild, spring, or stainless steel. As a rough guide, a strap made from 18 s.w.g. (1·2 mm) steel should prove suitable for bends up to 1½ inches (38 mm) thick, and 14 s.w.g. (2·0 mm) for any thicker material. Spring steel is used when the nature of the bend is such that the strap has to be twisted as well as bent. A hard, brittle steel should be avoided as it is unsuitable and dangerous for the operator; where possible a high-tensile steel should be used. The width of the strap should always be slightly greater than the width of the wood and all parts of the piece to be bent should be fully covered and supported.

If oak or other woods that are likely to stain in contact with steel have to be bent, it is advisable to line the inner side of the strap with a thin sheet of aluminium, or other suitable material, which can be bent loosely over the edges of the strap to hold it in place. Various methods of attaching the steel strap to the wood are employed, but by far the best is to provide the strap with wooden or metal blocks, usually referred to as end stops, and to fix or adjust these so that in the process of bending, the ends of the wood bear tightly on to them and the strap is held taut.

The forms around which the wood is to be bent may be made of wood or metal, the former being employed extensively for the simpler types of bends and where the number of bends of any one shape required is limited. Metal forms are usually employed for the production of complicated shapes and where a very large number of bends of the one shape are required. The advantages of using a metal form are that intermediate clamping is simplified, and the form will not lose its shape if it becomes necessary to dry and set the bends while clamped in position. It is advisable to cover the faces with a layer of metal such as 24 s.w.g. (0·56 mm) aluminium for easier cleaning and to facilitate the removal of bends from the forms.

Simple 'U' bend

In producing the common U-shaped and hairpin types of bend, it is usual first to locate and secure the mid-section of the wood and strap on the form and then to bend the two halves simultaneously around the form. The set-up for making such a bend in this manner is shown in *Plate 4* where it will be seen that the bending form is clamped in position on a table and the steamed specimen and strap located and secured to it by means of an air-operated ram. The strap is made taut initially by means of the adjustable metal end-stop. The bending operation is carried out by pulling the arms round to the final position shown.

It will be observed that the strap is fitted at both ends with back-plates which extend some distance along the back of the strap and are bolted firmly to the end-stops. The back-plates may be made of metal or wood and must be strong enough to counteract any tendency for the end-stops to rotate when pressure is applied. Without these plates the longitudinal forces transmitted by the wood to the strap tend to cause the end-stops to swivel in the manner illustrated in *Fig. 8*. This may result in the wood freeing itself from the strap, or, if prevented from doing this by the pull on the arms, it will most probably back bend in the manner shown. The importance of providing bending straps with some form of back-plate can hardly

FIG 5 *Bending between male and female forms*

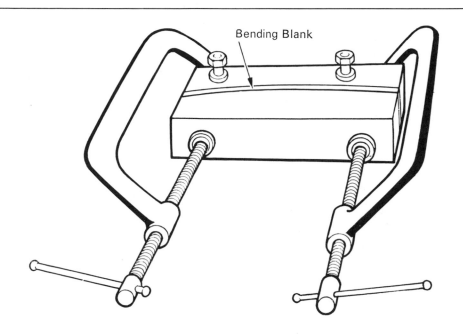

Bending Blank

FIG 6 *Bending over a metal form*

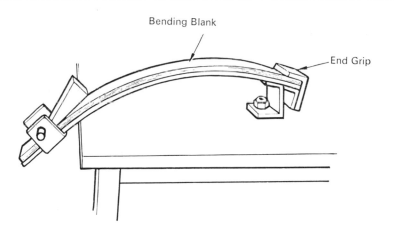

Bending Blank

End Grip

FIG 7 *Bending hoops*

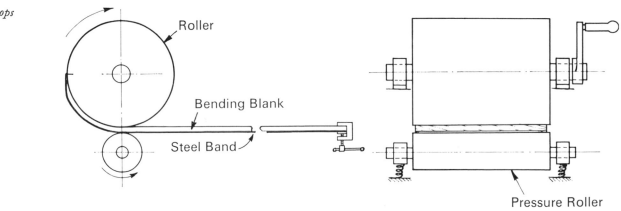

Roller

Bending Blank

Steel Band

Pressure Roller

FIG 8 *Bending with and without back plates*

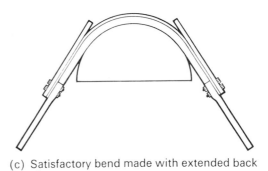

(a) Bend made without back plates showing the tendency to swivel.

(b) Bend made with back plates too short to be effective.

(c) Satisfactory bend made with extended back plates.

PLATE 4 *Set-up for making a simple U-shaped bend*

be overemphasized, and troubles encountered in practice are frequently attributable to their omission. The completed bend is held in position either by hand or, if necessary, by means of a clamp while some suitable tie-bar is being fixed across the ends to hold them in place for setting and drying.

A convenient clamping device for the temporary holding of the bend to the form consists of air clamps, the tops of which are flush with the table top during the bending operation and which may be caused to rise upwards immediately behind the strap at the conclusion of the operation, thus holding the ends in position. In the arrangement shown in *Plate 4*, the tie-bar used consists of an adjustable telegraph screw. Metal rods fitted at their ends with hooks or eyes which connect with corresponding eye-bolts or projections secured to the centre of the back end of the end-stops may be used in place of the telegraph screw. Once the tie-bar is in position, the bend, complete with strap and end-stops, back-plates and tie-bar, can be removed from the form for setting.

For many bends of this type it may be unnecessary to keep the strap in position during drying and setting, though the tendency for fractures to develop during this period is thereby considerably increased. However, it will still be necessary to tie the ends of the bend, and this may be done by nailing wooden strips across them, or by some such similar device. It will be necessary to nail strips both to the top and the bottom of the bent piece to overcome any tendency for the bend to twist on removal of the strap. Apart from the increased tendency for the bend to fracture in drying by removing the strap in this manner, the ends of the piece are often damaged as the result of nailing, and if more than one piece is bent in the one operation it becomes virtually impossible to secure strips on the top and bottom of each before removal of the strap, so that twisting is almost sure to result.

If the shape of the bend is not symmetrical, it will probably be found that on removal from the form appreciable change of shape will immediately take place when the simple forms of tie-bar already described are used. In such cases, it is necessary to clamp the bend to the form, or at least some portion of it, and to remove the clamped assembly to the drying room for setting.

When the piece to be bent has a small cross-section as compared with its length, there is always a tendency for the parts of the wood not yet in contact with the form to flex and bend away from the strap owing to the longitudinal pressure induced. As a result of this 'snaking' or 'back-bending', fractures are liable to occur, and the

finished bend will most likely be out of plane and distorted. It has already been explained that this tendency can be counteracted by the use of back-plates, but these alone are not always sufficient. A further possible method of minimizing such troubles is to allow the wood surface in contact with the strap to stretch a limited and controlled amount. The stretch must never be permitted to exceed about 2 per cent of the total length bent as otherwise tension failures will be present on the finished bend. This practice should only be adopted where absolutely necessary and, in general, any stretching of the fibres on the convex face should be avoided. To control extension of the wood the straps may be provided with adjustable end-stops as illustrated in Plate 4. With an end-stop of this type, the strap can be made to fit very tightly on the wood at the commencement of the bending operation, which is essential if the radius of the required shape is at all severe; the end pressures are controlled during bending by means of the hand-operated adjustment screw or preferably by means of a ratchet-type spanner.

Yet another method whereby back-bending or inadvertent distortions can be minimized, is by the use of vertical and horizontal clamps as illustrated in the set-up for making the ring-seat type bend (*Fig. 9*), but unless absolutely necessary, such additional equipment should be avoided if production rate is to be maintained as high as possible.

Where the type of completed bend is such that the strap cannot safely be removed and the support it offers dispensed with immediately without fear of fracture on the convex face, it will be advantageous to make the end-stop easily detachable. It is, however, important to keep detachable end-stops in position until a few fixing and holding clamps have been tightly fitted, otherwise the strap may slip along the wood causing tension failures to occur on the bend. Two types of adjustable and detachable end-stops are shown in *Figs. 10* and *11*.

Finally, it may be noted that if only a portion of the total length of a piece is to be bent and the rest has to remain straight, this can best be achieved and back-bending avoided by steaming and softening only that portion that needs bending. Steam chests or boxes can readily be fabricated into which furniture parts, for example, can be introduced so that only the central portions are in contact with the steam while the two ends are outside the steamer. This arrangement would be very suitable for the bows for the back of certain types of Windsor chairs and a localized steaming retort is illustrated in *Fig. 12*.

FIG 9 *Initial set-up of strap, clamps and adjustable end-stop for ring seat type bend*

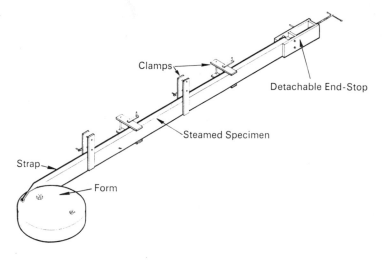

Clamps

Detachable End-Stop

Steamed Specimen

Strap

Form

FIG 10 *Detachable and adjustable end-stop*

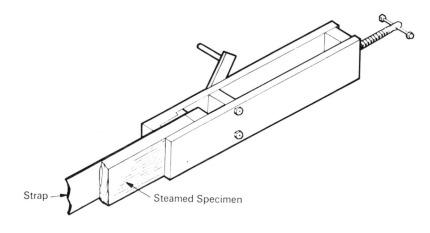

Strap

Steamed Specimen

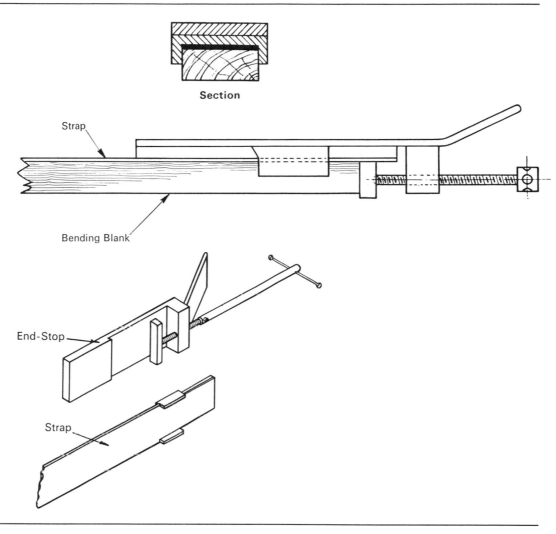

FIG 11 *Detachable and adjustable end-stop*

Section

Strap

Bending Blank

End-Stop

Strap

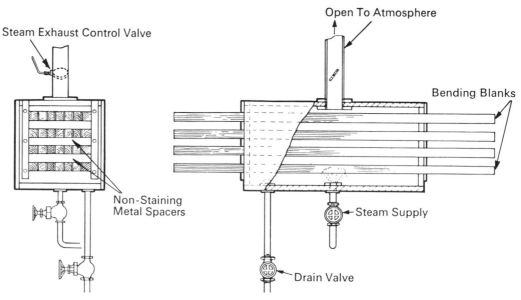

FIG 12 *Localized steaming retort*

Open To Atmosphere

Steam Exhaust Control Valve

Bending Blanks

Non-Staining Metal Spacers

Steam Supply

Drain Valve

Two-plane bends

For bends in more than one plane, the straps used must be arranged so that the bent parts of the wood are always covered on the convex face, irrespective of the plane of bending. A strap made on these lines is shown in *Fig. 13*, placed in position on a wood specimen prior to bending in two planes.

The first part of such a bend is effected in the normal manner, making use, if necessary, of intermediate clamps to minimize the risk of back-bending and to keep the wood within the limits of the strap. As soon as this part is completed it is clamped to the form and the end-stops removed. It is important to keep these end-stops in position until the fixing clamps are really tight, to prevent the strap slipping along the wood and causing tension failures on the bends. The two loose pieces of strap secured by metal angles at right-angles to the main strap, are next put in position along the wood and the released end-stops fitted to their ends. These straps are pulled tight by manipulation of the adjusting screws, and the two ends of the wood can then safely be bent in a plane at right-angles to the centre part as indicated in *Fig. 14*. Intermediate clamps may or may not be needed along the strap according to the nature of the wood, its dimensions, etc., but the finished bend is usually left clamped to the form and dried and set in this state.

A somewhat simpler, but effective, strapping arrangement for making bends in two planes is shown in *Fig. 15*. Here the centre portion only of the back-strap is made of continuous steel strip to which, as before, metal angles are attached to the ends. The end portions consist, however, of a series of short metal strips linked one to another (wire cable would serve the same purposes) so as to be free to swivel in the vertical plane. The secondary straps used for supporting the bend during the second part of the operation are secured to the metal angles on the ends of the centre portion of the main back-strap and also to the front of the end-stops. When the first part of the bend has been made and firmly clamped to the form, the end portions can immediately be bent in a plane at right-angles to the centre portion since the secondary straps are already in position and the linked ends of the main strap are able to adjust themselves to the curvature imposed in this direction. Since it is advisable to set the finished bends clamped to the form, metal forms are to be preferred to wood for most types of two-plane bends.

Re-entrant and S-type bends

When producing a bend in the form of an S it is usually necessary to secure two straps simultaneously to the piece to be bent, one to support each convex face. One method of making such a bend is to secure the forms to a base-plate in the correct relative positions and to fix to each one a separate strap. Each strap is fitted with an end-stop and the piece to be bent is laid in between, as shown in *Fig. 16*. The two ends are bent simultaneously and secured in position on the forms until dried and set. A variation of this method is to fit two long straps, one on either side of the piece, and to use these alternately, as illustrated in *Fig. 17*. Detachable end-stops are essential here, and after each part of the bend is made it is clamped securely between forms prior to the removal of the end-stop and the subsequent bending in the reverse direction. Re-entrant bends can be made by this method and a sinuous-type bend may be produced if the process is continued. Where the re-entrant bend has a comparatively large radius of curvature it is often possible to make it between male and female forms in the manner shown in *Fig. 18*. A bending strap is provided for the bends of smaller radius yet to be made, and this may be clamped between the specimen and the male form. As soon as the first part of the bend has been produced and the forms, wood and strap tightly clamped together, the end-stops on the strap are fitted to the ends of the specimen and these are bent in the normal manner. Here again it will be necessary to remove the complete set-up for drying and setting.

Chair-leg bends

Bends of comparatively large radius of curvature, suitable for chair legs, may be bent unsupported over metal forms in the manner already described, but when the curvature is such as to lead to fractures in bending it is necessary to provide the piece with a supporting strap. An arrangement such as that shown in *Fig. 19* is very suitable for this purpose; a modification of this method, employing a steam-heated form for quick setting, is shown in *Plate 5*.

One of the most complicated types of bend is that usually associated with the legs and back of the well-known Austrian bentwood chair. This is, in effect, a combination of the two-plane bend and the re-entrant. The straps used for this type of bend may resemble those used for the two-plane bend already referred to, and intermediate clamping devices are frequently employed. Normally, the back or top part is first bent to shape and tightly clamped to the form before any attempt is made to bend the legs proper. One leg is then bent at a time and two men are required for the operation. Experience

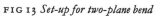

FIG 13 *Set-up for two-plane bend*

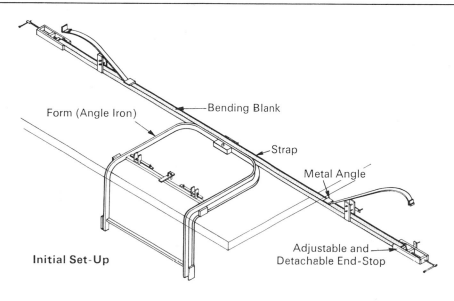

Form (Angle Iron)

Bending Blank

Strap

Metal Angle

Adjustable and Detachable End-Stop

Initial Set-Up

FIG 14 *Final stages in making a two-plane bend*

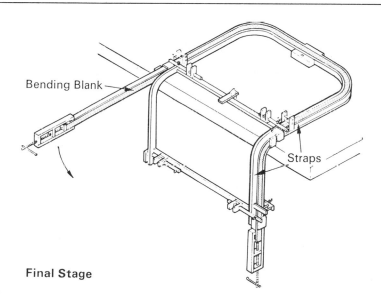

Bending Blank

Straps

Final Stage

FIG 15 *Strap with flexible linked system for making a two-plane bend*

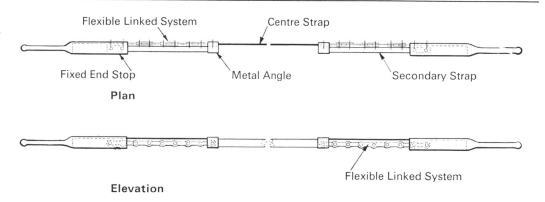

Flexible Linked System

Centre Strap

Fixed End Stop

Metal Angle

Secondary Strap

Plan

Flexible Linked System

Elevation

FIG 16 *'S'-type bend*

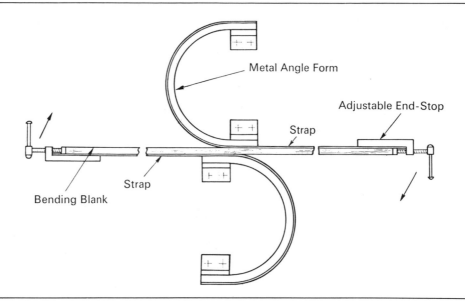

Metal Angle Form

Adjustable End-Stop

Strap

Strap

Bending Blank

FIG 17 *A method of making a sinuous type bend*

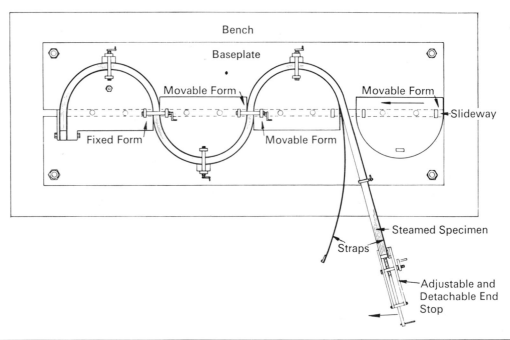

Bench

Baseplate

Movable Form

Movable Form

Slideway

Fixed Form

Movable Form

Steamed Specimen

Straps

Adjustable and Detachable End Stop

FIG 18 *A method of making a re-entrant type bend*

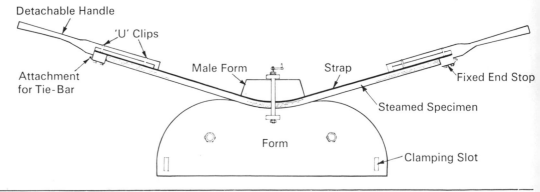

Detachable Handle

'U' Clips

Male Form

Strap

Fixed End Stop

Attachment for Tie-Bar

Steamed Specimen

Form

Clamping Slot

FIG 19 *A method of making a chair leg bend*

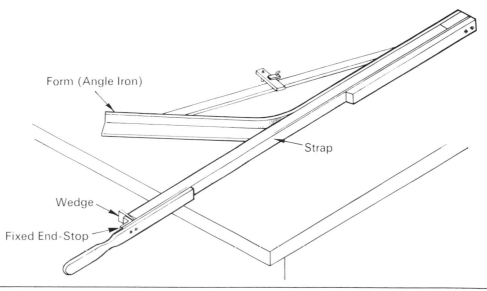

Form (Angle Iron)

Strap

Wedge

Fixed End-Stop

PLATE 5 *Steam heated metal form*

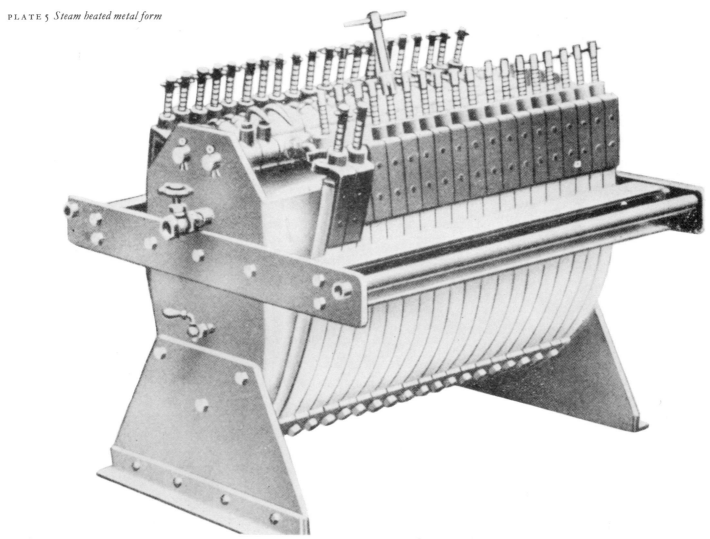

C

alone teaches the operators just where to place the intermediate clamps and when to remove them, and, indeed, success depends here almost as much upon correct clamping as upon other factors.

Transverse bending

It is not always realized that almost all woods may readily be bent in the transverse direction across the grain. However, wood is fissile and very prone to fracture when subjected to tensile stress across the fibres, and in making bends of small radii of curvature in this direction some support for the convex face is required. An example of the possibilities of this method is shown by spruce, which is considered to have inferior bending properties when bent in the direction of the grain, but may be bent across the grain, after immersion in boiling water, into the form of a tube having an internal diameter of $3\frac{1}{2}$ inches (90 mm) and a wall thickness of $\frac{1}{8}$ inch (3·2 mm) and, that without the support of a strap.

One method employed for making such a tube has been to clamp one edge of the panel to a heated steam pipe and then to steam the face away from the pipe so as to cause the piece to curve around it. After sufficient treatment, a strip of strong cloth or canvas is placed over the convex face to afford some mechanical support, and the whole slowly bent round the heated pipe until the required shape has been obtained. The bend is then dried and set before being removed from the pipe.

Steamed wood can be heavily compressed across the grain without fracturing, and the forces set up in bending are comparatively small.

Reinforcement

Most tropical timbers have inferior bending properties as compared with those from the temperate zones, mainly because they are incapable of sustaining more than a relatively small degree of compression before buckling and crumpling takes place. A method devised at the Forest Products Research Laboratory for improving their bending properties consists essentially of gluing to what is to be the compressed concave face a thin lamination of wood possessing good bending properties. This lamination is capable of supporting and reinforcing the contiguous layer of the poorer bending wood and inhibiting localized compressions and buckling, thus causing the maximum compressive strain to be increased considerably. Since all woods have better bending

properties across the grain than along the grain, the reinforcing layer can be made of a wood with poor bending properties provided it is laid with the grain at right angles to the rest of the piece. It is of course essential that the layers be joined together with a waterproof glue since they are to be subjected later to steam. The gluing technique involved can be essentially the same as that employed for making flat assemblies. The possibilities of this reinforcement technique are illustrated by the results of a Laboratory experiment with danta (*Nesogordonia papaverifera*). Under normal conditions a 1 inch (25 mm) thick sample of this timber, steamed and supported with a strap, has a limited bending radius of about 14 inches (360 mm). But composite material made up of $\frac{15}{16}$ inch (24 mm) danta supported by $\frac{1}{16}$ inch (1·6 mm) beech can be bent to a radius of about 6 inches (150 mm). Similar results have been obtained with guarea reinforced with a cross-banded layer of the same timber.

Built-up bends

Relatively thick bent parts having a radius of curvature considerably smaller than that shown in *Table 1* can be made by gluing together say two bends, one on top of the other. Each bend roughly half the thickness of the bent piece finally required, is steamed and bent separately with the aid of a metal strap. After setting and drying, the concave face of the one and the convex of the other need to be machined accurately so that they can be made to fit snugly together. Glue and the necessary lateral pressures are then applied to join the two pieces together. This method has been employed for making hockey stick head bends of very sharp radius and could be used also for bends of small radius with many of the tropical timbers that have intrinsically poor bending properties.

Cold bending after compression

(a) Pre-compressed wood

Precisely how heat treatments render wood compressible to a degree sufficient for bent work is not known, neither is it known why only certain species of timber are appreciably affected in this manner. Microscopic examination of fibres taken from the compressed face of a bend shows that the cell walls have buckled resembling a half-closed concertina. Numerous *slip planes* (dislocations of the cell wall due to compression) can be observed, yet no definite rupture or disintegration of the material as a whole has necessarily occurred. *Plate 6* shows a section of ash as seen under the microscope before and after steaming and bending, and the slip planes referred to are clearly visible. It needs to be pointed out, however, that in preparing sections for microscopic examination it is necessary to moisten the wood, which as a result tends to resume its initial dimensions, so the full extent of the compression induced in bending is not apparent in prepared sections.

Wood taken from near the concave face of a bend possesses properties differing considerably from those of the untreated material in its original state. In the cold state, heavily compressed wood shows considerable shrinkage and expansion in the longitudinal direction after limited drying or re-wetting but at high moisture content values, expansion tends to exceed shrinkage for a given moisture change, i.e. the wood tends to creep and ultimately resume its initial dimensions prior to bending. This tendency explains why, for example, the crook of a walking stick will flatten out if allowed to become very wet and will not return to its original shape when redried.

It has long been known also that compressed wood from the inside of a bend can become pliant and flexible in the cold state so that, if the compression is of considerable magnitude and the piece is not very thick, it may be bent and twisted quite readily between the fingers. Recently, the Laboratory has investigated the problem of producing what is called 'precompressed' and 'flexible' wood. The term 'precompressed wood' is used to denote material that has been steamed, compressed longitudinally and then the applied compressive force has been immediately removed. 'Flexible wood' has been further treated to induce a greater degree of pliability.

The chief difficulty in compressing long lengths of steamed wood is that the piece tends to buckle in the press, and if introduced into say, a strong metal support tends to compress heavily near the ends, causing the wood to jam and crush to breaking point.

The technical problem of compressing long lengths of wood without buckling has been solved with the aid of what might be termed the concertina-type of supporting device. This consists essentially of a series of square, metal-faced plates free to slide along retaining guide bolts and separated one from another by short, relatively light springs. In the centre of each plate is cut a hole of similar cross-section but very slightly larger than that of the piece to be compressed. This latter, after steaming, is inserted into the centre of the compressible support which is then placed in a press. Pressure is applied simultaneously to the piece and the supporting device so that both become compressed equally.

Material which is steamed and compressed longitudinally and immediately released does not regain its original length exactly and a small percentage of residual compression remains. The initial compression may be up to about 20 per cent of the original length for air-dried material of such species as beech, ash and elm, while residual strain may only be of the order of 3 or 4 per cent. Even so, this relatively small amount of residual strain is sufficient to provide a worthwhile reduction in the minimum radius of bend of the treated timber. No setting treatment is necessary after the compression and release process and as soon as the wood is cold it can be bent, at a moisture content as low as 12 per cent, to a smaller radius than matched steamed unsupported material. For example, 1 inch (25 mm) thick steamed beech has a bending radius of about 13 inches (330 mm) when unsupported, whereas matched compressed and released material can be bent to a radius of 9 inches (230 mm) at a moisture content of 12 per cent; if the moisture content is 18 per cent a radius of about 7 inches (180 mm) is attainable. The concertina-type device together with a sample of compressed wood are illustrated in *Plate 7*.

Several important advantages are to be gained by using precompressed wood. Machining and shaping operations can be undertaken and completed on straight material which can then be bent to shape in the cold state; this may enable machining operations to be carried out which would otherwise be considered too costly or too troublesome. Supporting straps can be dispensed with in certain instances, and beech bends 1 inch (25 mm) thick may be formed over the radius of curvature range of 13 inches (330 mm) to about 7 inches (180 mm) without them. Since the timber is cold and dry, even material of circular cross-section will suffer virtually no flattening during the bending operation. An appreciable reduction in the setting time of the bend may also be achieved where precompressed wood is used. For example, 1¼ inch (32 mm) diameter pieces of beech will take several hours to set to shape in a room at 66°C (150°F) after normal steam bending, but precompressed dry material can be set in about 2 hours under similar conditions. If radio-frequency heating is employed with a permeable species, such as beech, of these dimensions, setting can be achieved in 6 minutes i.e. 3 minutes heating at 100°C followed by about 3 minutes cooling.

This method of enhancing the bending properties of wood has proved to be of considerable importance, as is illustrated by the fact that there was an immediate practical application in the manufacture of the Y-D

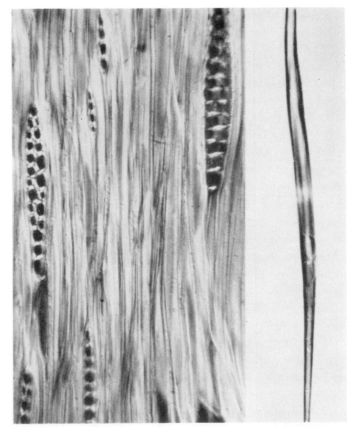

PLATE 6 *Photomicrographs of home-grown ash*

A *Untreated material (before steaming and bending)*

B *Material taken from the compression side of an ash bend*

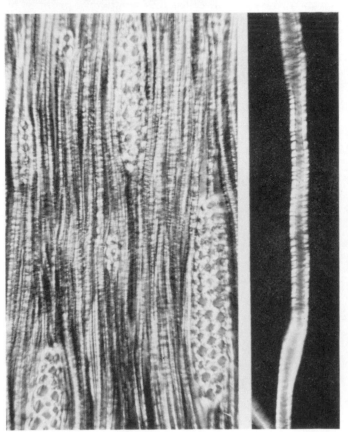

PLATE 7 *Concertina-type supporting device and sample of compressed wood*

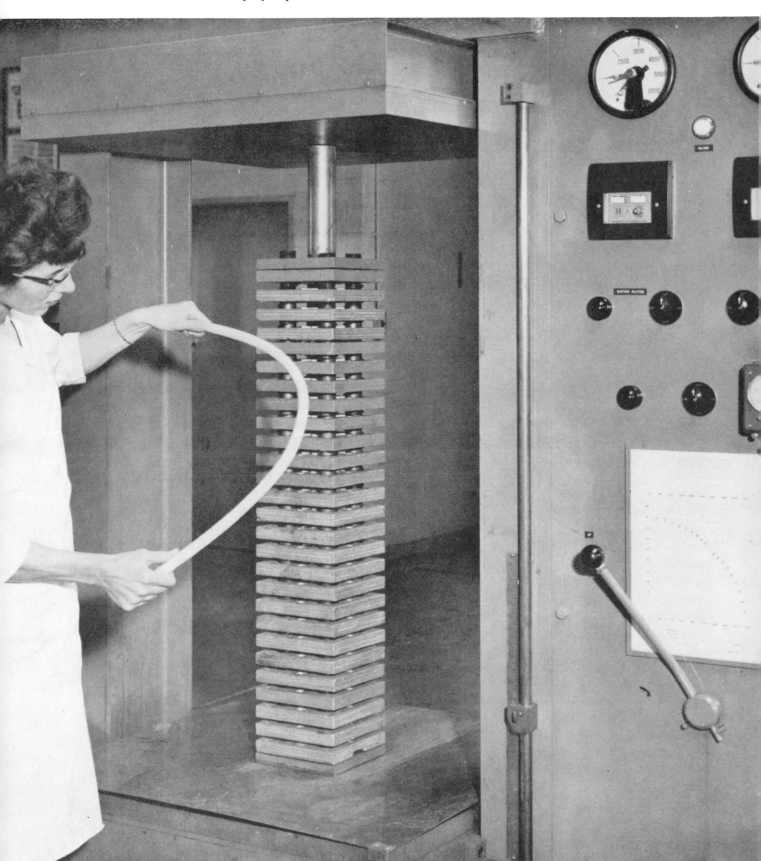

portion and the s-bend portion of spade handle shafts. The techniques described in the following chapter for producing these shafts involve a somewhat violent method of unsupported bending, and fractures are not uncommon. Now, however, by using precompressed wood, fractures have been reduced very considerably and in addition little sanding and cleaning of the handles is required since the shafts are bent in the unsteamed and freshly machined condition. In this particular application, of course, it is necessary to soften and compress only that portion of the shaft to be bent.

Other uses for this material have been in the furniture industry, in the production of chair legs and backs, also mouldings for table top rims. Precompressed specimens of beech 36 inches (910 mm) long, for use as chair legs, have been dried to a moisture content of 12 per cent and taper-turned and haunched and mortised before being bent to shape; similarly treated material for back rails has been band-sawn in width and spindle-moulded before bending.

This method of improving the bending properties of wood has so far only been found applicable to the good bending species such as elm, beech and ash. With the possible exception of such timber as guarea, danta and mansonia it is unlikely that the bending properties of tropical species can be enhanced to any appreciable extent.

(b) *Flexible wood*

If very flexible material is required it is necessary to induce in the wood still greater residual strains. Maximum pliability can be achieved by setting the heavily compressed material so that virtually the whole of the original strain is retained when the compressive force is removed. Beech, for example, might be induced to retain a residual strain of about 20 per cent without undue losses. To set the specimen in this fully shortened state within the concertina-type support is a somewhat protracted procedure; drying rates must inevitably be slow since the wood is almost completely enclosed and the process is unlikely to be economic.

Further research however has indicated that considerable flexibility can be achieved for a smaller residual strain than the 20 per cent mentioned above, and investigations have been carried out with a view to obtaining material with a rather lower but yet appreciable degree of residual strain.

One method devised for obtaining such material is to compress steamed wood to a strain of about 20 per cent of its original length and then release the load as for the production of precompressed wood. This material after being allowed to cool and dry can then be recompressed in the concertina jig in the cold state to a strain of about 20 per cent. On release of this second application of pressure a residual strain of the order of 15 per cent may be obtained in the wood which can subsequently be bent comparatively easily. Indeed experiments have indicated that 1 inch (25 mm) thick beech, after being subjected to the double-compression process can be bent to a radius of 4 inches (100 mm) in the cold dry state without the aid of a strap; this value closely approaches the minimum radius attainable with matched material steamed and strap-supported.

An alternative method where a slightly lower degree of flexibility is acceptable, is to compress fully the steamed wood and retain for a relatively short period the strain so induced, either by holding the supporting jig in the press or, more conveniently, by clamping the jig in the closed position, and removing it, together with the wood, for cooling. After a period of about an hour, the clamps can be removed and a residual strain of 12–15 per cent is retained in the wood; the clamping period can obviously be varied depending upon the degree of flexibility required. Flexible wood can be sawn and machined satisfactorily, although when turned in long lengths as for the production of, say, chair legs it may be necessary to introduce additional supports because of its extreme flexibility. Possible uses for this material are beading round curved windows, tennis racket crescents and two-plane bends for furniture. The methods described above for the production of precompressed and flexible wood have been patented.*

---

* Patent Nos. 965,451, 39280/63 and 1,101,137.

4 Machine bending

In whatever manner wood is bent, the principles underlying the process remain the same, but by the use of machinery, as distinct from the comparatively simple hand-bending equipment, a large number of bends can often be made in one operation, and the bending of large-dimension stock greatly facilitated. Production rates may be considerably increased, and, in addition, the lateral support provided when several pieces are bent side by side at the same time, reduces the tendency for distortional degrade to occur. Strictly speaking, the extended levers or handles fitted to the straps used in hand-bending methods might be considered machines or multiplying devices whereby greater forces may be exerted on the wood than would otherwise be possible. It is not usual, however, to regard them in this light and such equipment is seldom used for the production of multiple bends or bends of large dimensions.

Rope and windlass machine

Probably the simplest form of bending machine in the ordinary sense of the term consists of a hand- or power-driven winch linked by ropes or chains to the ends of the bending straps in the manner illustrated in *Plate 8*. For the initial set-up, the bending form is clamped to a bench, and to the centre of the curved part of this form is clamped the mid-section of the wood-strap system. In the arrangement shown, the strap is of simple design, fitted with wooden end-stops and back-plates. Wooden wedges have been inserted between the steamed bending blanks and the end-stops for tightening the strap. Guide pulleys are fitted along the length of bench joining the form and winch, and these are located in such a position that the ropes which pass round them exert a pull as nearly at right angles to the end-stops as possible, throughout the bending operation. By the operation of the winch, the two ends of the strap may then be pulled forward and towards one another so that the wood becomes wrapped tightly round the form.

In the particular set-up shown, the bend, when completed, was clamped securely to the form with the strap in position and the whole assembly removed to a drying room for setting the wood. The final drying would be accomplished with the strap removed and wooden tie-pieces nailed across the ends of each bend.

The alternative arrangement of fitting ropes or metal tiebars so as to connect the ends of the strap as soon as the bend had been made might have been adopted in preference to securing with clamps.

Lever-arm machines

The so-called lever-arm machines are essentially the same as the one already described, except that they are provided with stout metal levers or arms, by means of which the forces are transmitted to the wood-strap system. A machine of this type is shown in *Plate 9* and its similarity to the machine already described is readily apparent. In this machine there are in effect, two arms on either side of the centre line, and the top pair, to which is fitted the major strap, is connected to the bottom pair by means of struts pivoted top and bottom as shown in the illustration. The hydraulically-operated rams which control the power units are coupled directly with the lower pair of arms which when in operation cause the arms to thrust upwards as shown.

Initially the arms and the major strap are all horizontal and on top of this strap is put the minor one in which the steamed wood is to be placed. One end is provided with a fixed end-stop and at the other there is a steel plate fitted with three $\frac{5}{8}$-inch diameter (16 mm) studs, passing through the end-plate of the minor strap and bearing against an adjustable pressure-plate on the major strap. The wood is made to bear against this steel plate so that the end-pressures applied in bending are transmitted directly to the end-stop on the major strap by way of the studs. End pressure is applied before bending to make the major strap taut. On completion of the bending operation, there will inevitably be a gap between the end-plate on the minor strap and the back face of the steel plate that is bearing on the end of the wood. This gap must be bridged, and to do this the steel end-plate is provided with two $\frac{3}{4}$-inch (19 mm) bolts which can be screwed by hand to bear tightly on the surface of the minor strap end-stop. The tie-bar or holding-plate is fitted across the projections on these end-stops in the manner depicted and it remains only to release the major strap, return the arms to the horizontal position and pull the secured bent wood and strap from the bending form.

On the machine illustrated, provision has been made for pressure to be applied laterally when a number of relatively narrow pieces are bent side by side in one operation. This pressure is obtained by means of small pneumatically operated rams attached to the upper arms of the machine.

A modification of the above method is illustrated in *Fig. 20*. The framework consists essentially of (a) a stationary bed and (b) a sliding table free to move backwards and forwards along grooves in the stationary bed.

PLATE 8 *Bending wood by means of a winch*

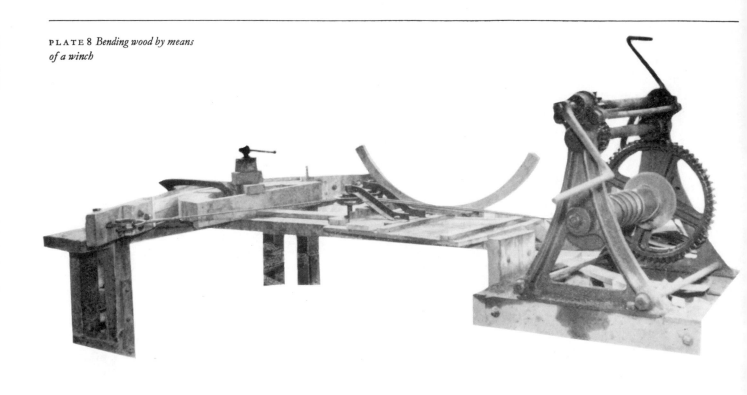

FIG 20 *A bending machine incorporating a hydraulic ram*

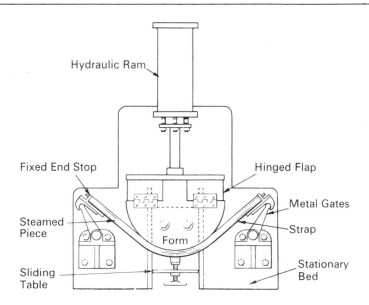

Hydraulic Ram

Fixed End Stop

Hinged Flap

Metal Gates

Steamed Piece

Strap

Form

Sliding Table

Stationary Bed

The bending form is secured to the sliding table and movement is imparted to it by means of a pneumatic or hydraulic ram.

On the fixed bed are secured two stout metal hinges or gates of suitable dimensions, separated by a distance approximately equal to the length of the wood to be bent. The metal straps are equipped with fixed end-stops and with metal back-plates extending slightly beyond the end-stops. On the backs of these plates, near their extremities, are cut semi-circular grooves which fit snugly on to the rounded ends of the metal gates on the stationary bed.

In the initial set-up the ram is at the back of its stroke, the wood is in position between the end-stops of the strap, and the rounded ends of the metal gates are fitted into the grooves of the back-plate. The bending form is then forced forward into the wood by the ram, and, since the ends of the strap are constrained to move only in the arc of a circle, the wood strap system is forced eventually to take up the shape of the form when the bending operation is completed. It remains to secure the ends of the strap by means of a tie-bar, withdraw the form slightly and remove the tied bend complete with strap for setting.

Revolving table machine

In this type of machine, one end of the wood and one end of the steel strap are both attached to a point on or near the bending form, which, in turn, is secured to a table or disc that can be rotated at will. A spring-loaded roller or other device for obtaining radial pressure on the back of the wood and strap at the point of contact with the form is normally provided. A long metal slide or feed arm is incorporated to constrain the end-stop on the metal strap remote from the form to move towards it at a tangent. When the table is revolved the wood and strap are automatically wrapped round the form and kept in close contact by pressure exerted radially by a spring or a pneumatically-operated ram.

A machine of this type used for making walking-sticks is shown in *Plate 10*.

In this machine the vertically-positioned revolving table turns anti-clockwise at a speed of about 1 rpm and in so doing pulls the wood-strap system along a series of metal rollers in a pivoted metal guide arm. At the table end, the end-stop on the strap is fixed but at the other end it is adjustable. The strap here is wide enough to take and bend eight walking stick blanks at a time.

Presses

Steamed wood is sometimes pressed to shape between male and female forms or cauls. Should a large hydraulic press be used in conjunction with a series of cauls, a considerable number of bends may be pressed in one operation and the whole battery may be clamped together and removed for setting.

Sometimes the press is provided with steam-heated cauls for quick setting as illustrated in *Plate 11*. In this set-up the bent pieces are left in the press until set to shape. If no supporting straps are used, the limiting radius of curvature must be comparatively large and great accuracy of shape cannot be obtained. It is, of course, possible to provide the wood with supporting straps if required, and an excellent machine of this kind for bending chair-back posts has been described and fully illustrated by T. R. C. Wilson of the Forest Products Laboratory, Madison, U.S.A.*

Spade handle bending machines

In making spade or shovel handles, bends may be required at one or both ends of the shaft. The end to be bent is first softened usually by immersion in boiling water or by steaming, after which the handle is securely gripped and held in position by means of a clamp, which may be allowed to slide freely in guides in the framework of the machine or may be fixed in position. In the production of the Y-D type handle the split ends are then forced into curved grooves in a steel or alloy form. Alternatively a two-piece form may be used and in this case the clamped handle remains stationary together with the female half of the form; the sliding male form is driven forward into the softened split ends of the handle which are consequently forced to the shape of the male and female forms (*see Plate 12*).

For certain types of handle an S-bend or swan-neck is required at the blade end and in making these, a split form is commonly used. The top half is kept in contact with the bottom half during the bending operation by means of a wedge clamp. The top portion of each form is slightly deeper than the lower one and both are grooved and shaped to the required contour of the bend. The slide carrying the form is driven forward and the firmly held softened wood is forced into it and made to conform to the shape required (*see Plate 13*).

---

* Bending Wood Stock. Wood Working Industries, November 1929.

PLATE 9 *Lever arm bending machine*

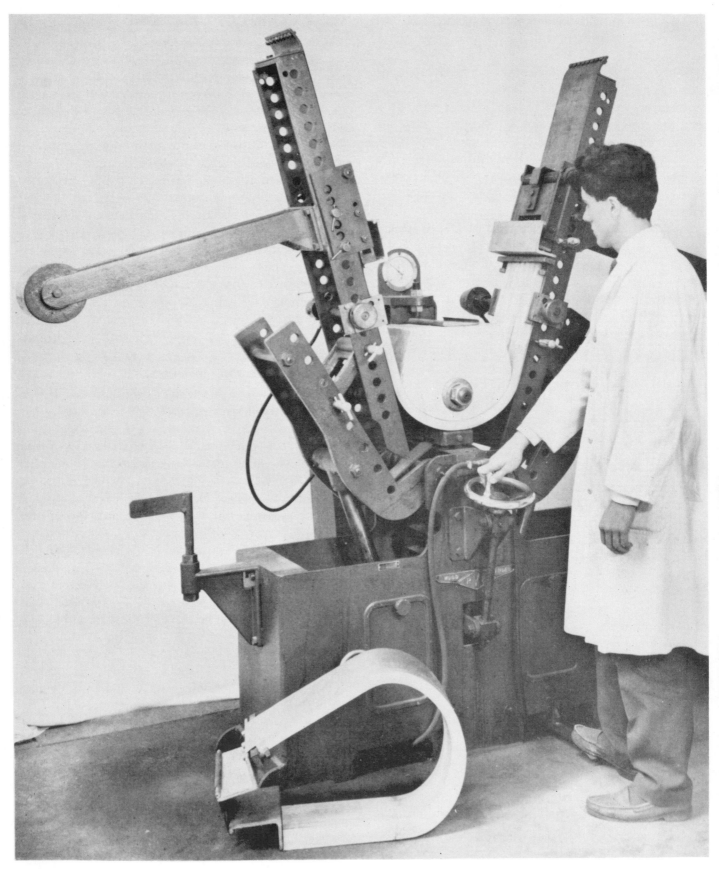

PLATE 10 *Revolving table bending machine*

PLATE II *Hydraulic press and steam-heated cauls*

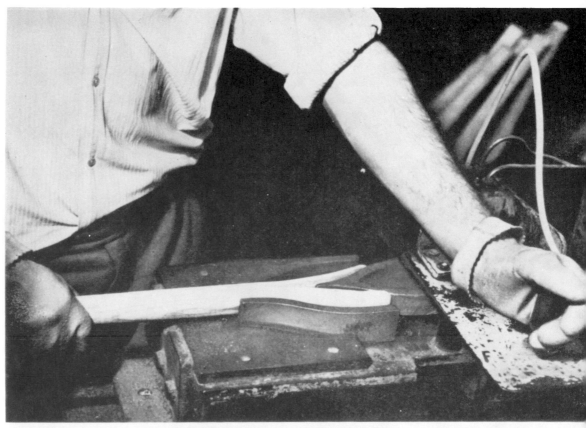

The handles encased in the appropriate forms are then taken to a warm room or placed over steam-heated pipes, and the wood allowed to set to shape. As soon as the bent portion has re-dried and set, the metal forms are removed and the completed handles are ready for assembly.

Cooperage

The art of making tight casks or barrels for holding liquids is one of great antiquity, demanding the greatest skill and care since, in addition to being perfectly leak-proof, the vessels must bear the strain of transportation and may have to resist considerable internal pressure if they contain fermenting liquors. There are, of course, several types of barrel for holding a variety of liquids, and the species of timber used and methods employed for their manufacture are not all the same. For example, in the herring industry, softwood staves are commonly used and made ready for bending by heating over a wood fire. In the brewing industry, however, steam is used for the softening process and machinery usually employed for the actual bending operation.

Probably one of the most important operations in making barrels is the shaping of the staves, which in the brewing industry are usually made from well-seasoned quartered oak and are so fashioned that finally it is only necessary to bend them in one direction to obtain the shape of the barrel. Each stave is usually machined to exact profile and has an increase in width from the ends to the middle, a bevel on each edge, and is curved on the faces˙ which finally form the inner and outer surfaces of the finished barrel.

In the process of assembly, a number of staves are selected and these, one by one, are stood on end and their top ends fitted within a metal hoop. When a sufficient number of staves have been arranged in this manner another hoop of larger diameter is slipped over the assembly and forced along the staves, drawing them tightly together so that at this stage the assembly resembles roughly a truncated cone with the bottom ends of the staves splayed outwards. The assembly of staves with the two hoops in position is then taken to a steaming box, which may consist of a base-plate fitted with an open-ended steam pipe and a bell-shaped metal top of rather larger dimensions than the stave assembly. The metal top or hood can be raised well clear of the base-plate so as to accommodate the assembly, which is placed over the centrally situated steam pipe. As soon as the top is lowered to form a reasonably steam-tight chest, the steam is turned on and the staves subjected to a suitable softening treatment. Immediately after the treatment, the assembly is removed to a bending machine which frequently consists essentially of a rope and windlass and some mechanism for forcing additional metal hoops into position. The rope is wrapped round the splayed bottom ends of the staves in such a way that when tightened by means of the windlass these ends are pulled inwards and drawn together. Metal hoops of varying diameters are then, one by one, placed over the assembly and forced into position mechanically, thus binding and forcing the staves still tighter together until the required size of barrel has been obtained. Once the strain is taken by the hoops the rope may be released, and it then remains to cool and dry the wood for the proper setting of the staves to shape. Other operations connected with the fitting of the heads, permanent hoops, etc., are finally carried out before the barrel is completed.

5 The setting of bends

Setting techniques

It has been shown in a previous chapter that tensile and compressive strains are induced in the material during the bending process, and that unless these are kept within certain limits they may cause fractures to occur. Unless the bent material is held in restraint residual stresses will cause a piece of bent wood to open out and return approximately to its former shape. If, for example, the clamps or tie-bars holding a bend to shape are removed immediately after the bending operation, movement of the ends of the bend in an outward direction will almost invariably occur. The distance moved will depend on several factors, such as the moisture content and species of timber, radius of curvature etc., and such movement will continue until the residual forces are of insufficient magnitude to overcome the stiffness of the piece as a whole. During the bending process, the material is usually strained beyond its elastic limit so that some permanent deformation of the fibres occurs. For this reason a bend that is allowed to move seldom returns completely to its former shape. When, however, the induced strains are below the elastic limit, removal of all restraint results in almost complete removal of the strain in the fibres and hence the piece will return very nearly to its original shape.

In order, therefore, to cause a piece of bent wood to retain its curvature, it is essential either to reduce the magnitude of the latent stresses causing movement, to increase the stiffness, or to employ a combination of the two. This process is referred to as *setting*, but it does not follow that because a bend is set to shape it is necessarily perfectly dry and ready for incorporation in the finished article.

Setting can be accomplished most readily by removing some of the moisture and by cooling the bend, and in some respects may be considered as a reversal of the softening treatment where the wood is heated under moist conditions. Though moisture is a factor in the setting process, it is not necessary that a bend should be dried down to any particular moisture content before becoming set. In fact, when green timber has been used in making a bend it may be found after cooling to be set approximately to the shape of the form on which it was made, even though the average moisture content of the bend after the setting process is still high and in excess of the fibre-saturation point.

Since, ideally, before a bend is incorporated in the finished product it should be both set and dried to the appropriate moisture content in service, it is apparent that further drying of such bends after the setting process becomes necessary. This further drying will be accompanied by a change in shape of the bend, as will be explained later. When, therefore, accuracy of shape is essential, it is recommended that the bend should first be set, then conditioned in the workshop and finally machined to exact profile.

The setting process may be considerably accelerated by subjecting the bend to hot, dry air, and a temperature of about 66°C (approx. 150°F) is commonly used. In some instances temperatures as high as 88°C (approx. 190°F) can be used without damaging the material. Setting rooms are usually designed after the fashion of a simple drying kiln incorporating steam-heated pipes, although any warm store would be equally suitable for the purpose, especially if provision is made for removing the moist air. It is seldom necessary to control the air humidity in a setting room.

During the setting process a bend must always be held to shape and if removed from the bending form, which will of course speed up the setting, must be held by means of nailed strips, tie-bars or similar attachments. In some instances it may be found safe to remove the strap immediately after the bending operation, but usually when a bend is hot and wet it is liable to fail subsequently in tension, particularly when the grain is not absolutely straight, even though faultless when removed from the bending form. Straps, if possible, should therefore be left on the bend for part, if not all, of the setting period, and should preferably not be removed until the bend has cooled.

Definite periods of setting cannot normally be given since they will be dependent on several factors, such as room temperature, dimensions, radii of curvature, moisture content of stock, etc., and it will generally be found necessary to carry out a few preliminary tests to determine the most suitable period for any particular bend. A very rough indication of how far setting has advanced however, can usually be obtained by visiting the setting room at intervals and testing the tightness of clamps, tie-bars, etc.; when these are loose to the touch it can be assumed that the bend is set. As an approximate guide, it may be said that $1\frac{1}{4}$ inch $\times$ $1\frac{1}{4}$ inch (32×32 mm) air-dried material bent to a radius of 9 inches (230 mm), may be set at a temperature of 66°C (approx. 150°F) in about nine hours; if allowed to cool for about one hour and then removed from the strap, the bend should be ready for use after a period of about two days' storage under workshop conditions.

Bends made from green material may be set in a similar manner but, as already explained, greater risks attend such a process if the timber is relatively impermeable, and a longer period than given above must necessarily elapse before the wood is thoroughly conditioned. Lower setting temperatures can, of course, be used, and in certain cases are to be recommended, as when, for example, strength characteristics of the finished product are of primary importance, or the material is likely to collapse or in any other way suffer from the rapid drying at higher temperatures.

Sometimes bent wood components, especially in small cross-sectional dimensions, can be incorporated in a finished article before they are fully dried without causing serious trouble in use, but the extent to which such deviation from the ideal is permissible is a matter for the practical man to decide from his own experience. Finally, it should be noted that when the strains induced in making a bend are largely within the elastic limit of the material, as in bends of comparatively large radius of curvature, the bend nearly always tends to straighten out somewhat when freed from restraint, even though thoroughly dried. It is usual, therefore, to bend such pieces initially to a rather smaller radius than is required, to allow for subsequent alteration in curvature. Furthermore, in view of the difficulty of holding certain bends of large radius to shape during the setting process, it is preferable to make and set them on heated metal forms in the manner already described. If the forms are heated by steam, a minimum period of three hours, for air-dried stock of approximately 1¼ inch by 1¼ inch (32 × 32 mm), is necessary to achieve a reasonable final shape.

Alternative form-heating techniques are sometimes considered worthwhile to achieve further reduction in the setting period, and one of these is to heat the curved surface of the form by means of an electrical heating element. The setting period will of course depend on several factors, including the species, dimensions and initial moisture content of the material, and care must be taken to control the form temperature so as to avoid scorching the surface of the bend. Preliminary tests will need to be carried out, but some idea of the greatly reduced setting time can be obtained from the fact that air-dried pieces of beech can be set to the shape of a Windsor bow (minimum radius of curvature approximately 5 inches (127 mm) using a form temperature of 149°C (300°F) and heating period of 15 minutes; a cooling time of about 15 minutes is required before the bend is fully set and is removed from the form.

Very considerable reduction in setting periods can be obtained by heating bends to about boiling point using radio-frequency heating. However, this usually involves the generation of steam within the cells, which may produce internal splitting and checking in many of the commonly used bending timbers, in some cases even in the normally permeable structure of beech. As a means of setting therefore, it appears unlikely that the method will be used in practice often. In the setting of bends made from precompressed or flexible wood, however, trouble is less likely to occur when using a permeable species such as beech due to the lower initial moisture content, and the process has been successfully employed for the setting of 1¼ inch (32 mm) round section beech chair leg bends. A setting period of three minutes is required compared with the two hours necessary to set similar bends in a room maintained at 66°C (approx. 150°F). With impermeable species, however, even though the moisture content may be of the order of 12 per cent, internal rupture of the cell walls is liable to occur at radio frequency inputs necessary to afford an appreciable saving in time.

The movement or change in shape of bends

Bends of comparatively small radius do not open out to the same extent when dried and, in fact, bends of very small radius frequently turn inwards when released owing to the natural shrinkages that have occurred during drying. If the bend has been thoroughly dried, it will take up its final position as soon as it is freed from restraint and subsequent movements will not necessarily be appreciable unless it is subjected to abnormal changes in atmospheric conditions. Fluctuating atmospheric conditions affect bent wood rather more than a piece cut to shape, for not only are there the same consequent changes in cross-sectional dimensions which in themselves account for changes in the radius of curvature, but also longitudinally compressed wood shows an increased tendency to shrink and expand in the direction of the grain. An increase in moisture content will cause the radius to increase, and similarly a decrease will cause the radius to decrease.

There is also a latent tendency for a bend to straighten out, and if it is subjected to high humidity conditions for a long period it may open out considerably and not return exactly to its original shape and curvature when re-dried. If the bend becomes very wet indeed, particularly at high temperatures it may open out very appreciably if unsupported, and if held at the ends it may actually break. Such troubles are not common in this country, but are not infrequent in tropical climates where every effort should be made to make the bends as impervious to moisture as possible and to keep them dry by artificial means in so far as this is practicable.

Part B: Laminated bends

6 The process of laminated bending

General considerations

It is well known that all timbers can be bent to a certain extent in the cold state without fracturing, and that very thin strips may easily be bent to a small radius of curvature. Pieces so bent, however, owing to their elastic properties, will tend to resume their original shape upon removal of the bending force unless they are secured and held to shape in some way. Such support or fixing may be afforded by firmly securing the bent pieces to a rigid framework, or by securing a number of concentrically bent pieces one to another in such a manner that relative movements are rendered virtually impossible. This latter method, known as laminated bending, is considered in this chapter. The technique first to be described are primarily concerned with the bending of laminations for other than structural purposes, such as in the furniture, sports goods, coachbuilding industries etc. In view of the increasing importance of the application of laminated bends for structural purposes, however, some details of the specialized techniques involved and relevant data are included in Chapter 8.

In laminated bending, relatively thin wooden strips or laminations are assembled adjacent to each other with the grain approximately parallel, and all are bent simultaneously over a single bending form. No restraint is imposed on the ends of any one lamination, which is free to slide over a contiguous piece during the bending process. The completed bend thus consists of a series of individually bent laminations which are usually secured one upon the other by means of glue on adjacent faces. The individually bent pieces are no longer free to slide over each other when the glue has set and relative movement is in this manner so restrained that virtually no further alteration in shape can occur, and the bend as a whole thus becomes set and fixed to shape.

Advantages of laminated bending are as follows

1 thick bends of small radius can be built up from thin laminations of any species of timber whatsoever;
2 poor quality timber containing knots, splits and other defects which would render the wood quite unfit for solid bending may, within reason, be incorporated;
3 if the laminations are sliced or rotary cut, considerable saving in timber may be effected compared with solid bending (conversely of course, appreciable loss may be occasioned if thin laminations are prepared by sawing);
4 long lengths may be obtained by the end jointing of shorter pieces by scarfing or other means and if the

joints are properly made and staggered in the completed bend, no appreciable weakening of the cross section need result;
5 laminated bends can usually be set more readily and made to conform better to the shape of the form than similar bends of solid material;
6 no softening treatment is generally required before the pieces are bent.

Disadvantages of laminating are

1 rather more technical skill and better equipment are usually required than for solid bending;
2 the presence of glue may be somewhat detrimental to the machines used for the final cleaning up of the bent pieces;
3 the glue lines which are usually visible on the sides may be objected to for aesthetic reasons;
4 the production of laminated bends in more than one plane presents greater difficulties than are encountered in the method of solid bending;
5 the preparation of the pieces for gluing, the drying of the timber by artificial means, and cutting of the laminations etc., usually result in a higher cost for the laminated product.

Selection and preparation of laminations

In preparing material for the production of laminated bends, the methods used are much the same as those employed in making flat laminated assemblies. It is, however, particularly important when preparing material for bent members to ensure that each individual lamination is of uniform thickness, since the methods normally employed in pressing together glued laminations do not permit the use of very high pressures, and any appreciable variation in thickness may result in thick glue lines and hence poor strength properties. No piece containing any form of decay should be used, since it will almost certainly be found to be extremely brittle. Laminations should be dried to a moisture content appropriate to the conditions of use, and in general a value of less than 20 per cent is required before satisfactory adhesion can be obtained; the individual members may be in the form of sawn, sliced or rotary-cut veneers or plywood.

It is uncommon, except in the manufacture of structural members and ships' timbers, to incorporate laminations more than about $\frac{1}{8}$-inch ($3 \cdot 2$ mm) in thickness, but in selecting the thickness of laminations to be used one of the most important factors to be considered is the limiting

PLATE 14 *Examples of laminated bends used in industry*

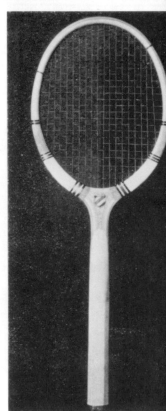

radius of curvature to which the wood can be bent without fracture occurring. An indication of these radii for laminations of ⅛-inch (3·2 mm) thickness or less, for several different species of wood is given in *Table 2*. This information has been compiled from the results of tests carried out at the Forest Products Research Laboratory and indicates the radius of curvature to which certain laminations may be bent so that not more than 5 per cent of the total number of bent pieces will fracture during the process. The values relate to good quality straight-grained material free from all defects such as pin knots, etc. bent in the cold, dry state round unheated forms with the grain of each lamination parallel to the length of the piece. It will be observed that there is considerable variation between species and the ratio of radius of curvature to thickness varies from 31 for rock elm and Dutch elm to 87 for opepe. In general, laminations obtained from the temperate hardwoods can be bent to smaller radii than those of the same thickness obtained from softwoods, and temperate hardwoods are in general superior to tropical hardwoods.

Tests carried out to date to investigate the effect of such variables as the direction of the annual growth rings relative to the axis of curvature, rate of growth, method of conversion, i.e. rotary, sliced or sawn, etc., on the limiting radii or curvature, have indicated that these factors generally have a negligible effect. If fractures are to be avoided when sliced or rotary-cut pieces are used in bends, it is important to ensure that the loose face of the material is on the concave face of the bend, and therefore in compression during the bending process. The effect that the position of the loose face has on the limiting radii of curvature for three different species may be seen from *Table 3*.

As in the case of thicker solid timber, the bending properties of thin, dry material may be improved, and the limiting radii of curvature reduced, by increasing the moisture content and/or increasing the temperature of the wood.

Glues

Almost any type of glue may be used and, in making a choice, such factors as cost, speed of setting, moisture resisting properties, etc., must be considered. For furniture work, animal or casein glues may be satisfactory although synthetic resin adhesives are being increasingly used. Urea formaldehyde adhesives offer a considerable measure of resistance to moisture and have been used for example in sail-plane constructional work, boats and caravans etc. For highly stressed members, however, under more exacting exposure conditions of moisture and high temperature the phenolic or resorcinol types of adhesive are to be preferred and their use is discussed in some detail later. In general, a glue having gap-filling properties is desirable for laminated work. The gluing technique to be adopted for the production of laminated bends is in all essentials the same as that for flat material. Detailed information of the procedure to be adopted in using any particular make of glue should be obtained from the manufacturers, and it is not proposed here to deal with the subject in any detail. It will suffice to say that in gluing it is always essential to apply uniform and adequate pressure to the assembly until the glue has set, in order to obtain satisfactory bonding of the laminations.

Pre-bending

In certain instances, where a bend of comparatively small radius of curvature is required, it may prove uneconomic or inconvenient to use laminations so thin that they may be bent in the cold, dry state without fracture. In such cases it is necessary to improve the bending properties of the wood as far as possible by the application of heat and moisture and to bend the laminations roughly to shape. The most convenient way of softening the wood is by immersing the laminations in boiling water for a period long enough to heat the material right through to the centre. In this way the limiting radius of all timbers, including softwoods, may be considerably reduced, as shown in *Table 4*. It is difficult to obtain satisfactory glue adhesion to wood surfaces which are above a moisture content of about 20 per cent. Pieces subjected to this softening treatment are bent approximately to the shape required and held until set. Then, if over 20 per cent moisture content they are re-dried and glue is spread on these preformed laminations and the final assembling and pressing carried out in the normal manner to be described in *Chapter 7*.

7 Pressing laminations to shape

The following are some of the more commonly used methods of bending laminated assemblies to shape for the production of bends of relatively small dimensions.

Male and female forms

The laminations may be pressed between shaped male and female forms as shown in *Fig. 21*. The pressure may be applied by screws or clamps and must be sufficient to conform with the gluing specification laid down by the makers of the particular adhesive used, making due allowance for the extra pressure required for the actual bending of the material.

Air clamps or hydraulic presses may be employed, and in the latter case it is usually found convenient and economic to prepare a series of forms so as to press a number of assemblies simultaneously. The pressure imposed may then be maintained by means of screw clamps and the whole pack, tightly held and secured, removed in one unit for setting so as to free the press for further work. The arrangement is illustrated in *Fig. 22*.

Forms are usually made of wood and should be well covered with anti-adhesive paint or coating, but metal forms may also be used.

Obviously, the male and female forms must be cut accurately to shape if pressure variations from point to point along the length are to be kept to a minimum.

An alternative to the female form is a metal band provided with tightening screws for exerting pressure as shown in *Fig. 23*.

Both these methods, however, are open to the objection that greater pressure must be exerted at the vertex of the bend than at the ends. This objection can, to a certain extent, be overcome by splitting the male and female forms into a number of segments and clamping each independently as in *Fig. 24* or by applying radial pressure at a number of points to a flexible band acting in place of the female form. Such an arrangement is shown in *Fig. 25* where the band consists of a number of thin wooden strips pre-bent roughly to the shape required. Radial pressure is applied in this case by means of wedges, though other suitable clamping devices might be used.

Fluid pressure

The best method of applying uniform pressure over the complete surface area of a bend is by means of fluid pressure. One way of doing this is to incorporate a flexible hose or tube between one form and the laminated assembly. After bending the glued laminations and securing the forms in the required relative positions, the tube is inflated by means of air or water until the desired pressure is read on the gauge (*see Fig. 26*). By this means pressure is applied radially and uniformly along the complete length of bend and only one form need be cut accurately to shape. Usually, though not always, it is the male form that is employed as a mould, since the bending operation is performed more easily round a convex mould than inside a concave one. In certain instances, however, an expanding rubber hose or bag may take the place of the male form, in which case the laminated assembly is first bent by hand approximately to the shape of the female form and then pressed tightly to exact shape by fluid pressure (*see Fig. 27*).

In a similar manner a rubber sheet or bag may take the place of the female form and *Fig. 28* shows a set-up in which the laminations and mould are placed inside a rubber bag and bent and pressed to shape by exhausting the bag of air so as to subject the wood to atmospheric pressure of about $14\,\text{lbf/in.}^2$ ($0 \cdot 10\text{N/mm}^2$). For the proper bending and bonding of thicker laminations, such a pressure is often insufficient, in which case it may be augmented by placing the bag, mould and laminated assembly in an autoclave or pressure cylinder. Here, as before, the air is exhausted or allowed to escape from under the rubber, and air at pressures higher than atmospheric is applied to the top side; virtually any desired pressure may thus be applied normal to the surface of the bent part.

Production of continuous laminated shapes

Various techniques are available for making continuous wooden shapes such as hoops, coffee table rims, seat rings, tambourines, sieves and steering wheels etc. Elaborate processes are sometimes involved but the methods which are now described require relatively simple equipment.

(a) *Split female form*

A female type form is used, shaped internally to the outside diameter of the hoop required. The form is made in two halves which are mounted on slides so that they can be forced together or separated by means of rams, screw-cramps or other means.

The laminations with the glue applied and with the ends cut square to a predetermined length are coiled one

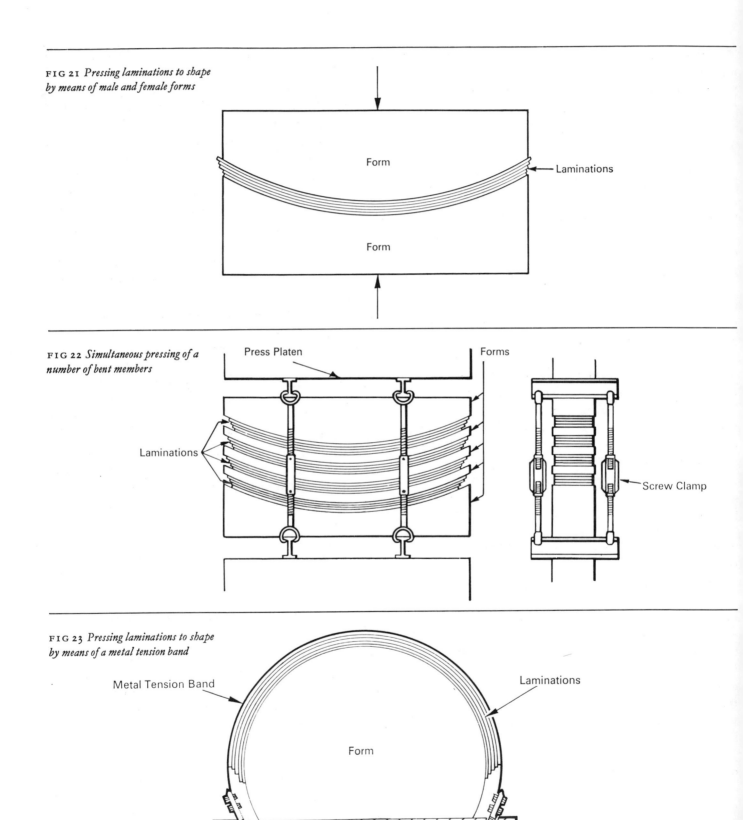

FIG 21 *Pressing laminations to shape by means of male and female forms*

Form

Laminations

Form

FIG 22 *Simultaneous pressing of a number of bent members*

Press Platen

Forms

Laminations

Screw Clamp

FIG 23 *Pressing laminations to shape by means of a metal tension band*

Metal Tension Band

Laminations

Form

FIG 24 *Pressing laminations to shape by means of split female forms*

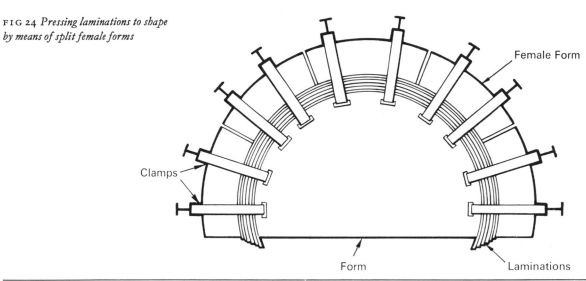

Female Form

Clamps

Form

Laminations

FIG 25 *Pressing laminations to shape by means of pre-bent wooden strips and wedges*

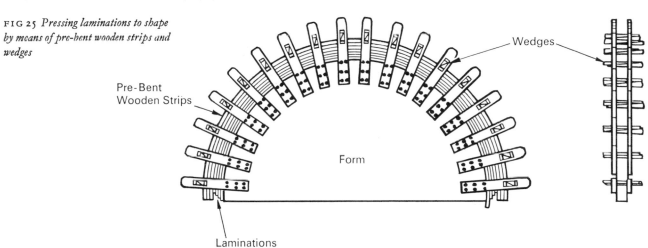

Wedges

Pre-Bent Wooden Strips

Form

Laminations

FIG 26 *Pressing laminations to shape by means of an inflated flexible rubber hose and a metal strap*

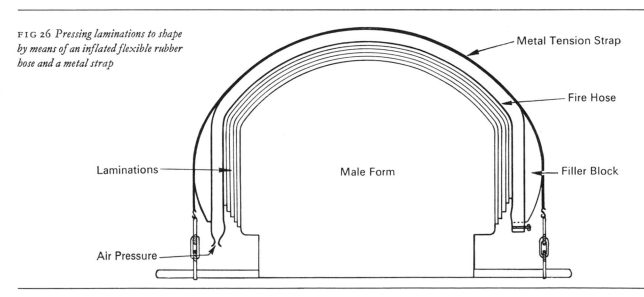

Metal Tension Strap

Fire Hose

Laminations

Male Form

Filler Block

Air Pressure

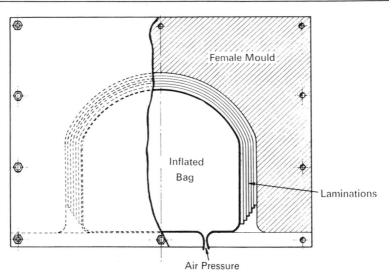

FIG 27 *Pressing laminations to shape by means of an inflated rubber bag and female mould*

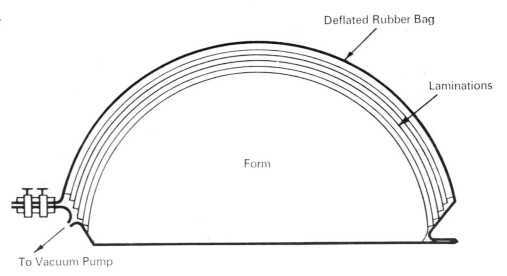

FIG 28 *Pressing laminations to shape by means of a deflated rubber bag*

at a time in the open mould in the correct order, care being taken to ensure that the joints are staggered. When the two halves of the mould are forced together, the butting of the ends of the laminations on the extreme inner face is made to induce a radial pressure in the glue layers which is adequate for efficient adhesion. This method has been used for making shells of tambourines. For more exacting requirements the laminations are all cut to length with scarfed ends and are pressed more firmly and accurately to shape with the aid of an inflatable hose or rubber bag fitted within the assembled laminations and round a circular male form; in this case the female form is used in the closed position, or it may be made in one piece. In an alternative method a circular male form shaped to the internal diameter of the required hoop is located at the centre of the split female form. The scarfed laminations are coiled in position as already described and the necessary gluing pressure applied by forcing together the two halves of the split form. After setting, the hoop and male form are removed and the laminated assembly is forced from the latter by a ram or some other means. The hoops can be made in widths as required and glue setting may be very considerably accelerated by employing low-voltage strip heating elements round the inside of each half of the split female form (*see Plate 15*), or radio-frequency heating may be used.

Such a process is often used in the manufacture of wooden-rimmed steering wheels. The completed hoop, which may be say, 4 inches (100 mm) deep and made up of 2 mm or 3 mm laminations, is sliced into four rings just under an inch (25 mm) deep, and each provides rims for one steering wheel. These pieces are split into two, and each half is rebated to accommodate the outer rim of the metal spider, which is then bonded between the wooden members with a resorcinol resin type adhesive. The wheel is then rounded off and finger grips cut into the underside. Reinforcing rivets are sometimes used to additionally secure the rims to the spider or for decorative effects.

(b) *Revolving form and tension strap*

A wooden or metal form (circular or otherwise shaped according to the hoop required) is mounted on a table that can be revolved by hand; a number of laminations are clamped to the form, one on top of the other, sufficient to build up the required thickness and just not thick enough individually to fracture when bent. The length of each in the completed bend has to be calculated accurately and the inner and outer laminations are scarfed at the ends. The inner ones may be cut to a length rather less than that

required to make a perfect butt joint and the resulting gaps can be filled by inserting wooden wedges. One end of each lamination must be made to fit approximately to the shape of the form, and it will usually be necessary to pre-bend the ends; this may be done by moistening them and pressing between heated male and female forms. These moulds can be made of wood, and low-voltage strip heating enables the ends to be set in a matter of a few seconds. After pre-bending the ends, the glued laminations are clamped to the form with a spring steel strap placed over the outer one. Radial pressure is applied by means of an air ram and roller, and by revolving the table and form the laminations are wound to the required shape. The whole assembly including the form can now be removed from the table, and as soon as the glue is set the finished bend can be forced free ready for cleaning, machining and final use.

(c) *The continuous strip method*

In this process, which was developed at the Forest Products Research Laboratory, laminations of the required width, scarfed at each end, are prepared at a moisture content of about 15 per cent. It is essential that the scarfs should be smooth and accurately made, and any reasonable length of piece may be used from practically any timber species; the thickness is limited only by the bending properties of the timber and the radius of bend. The prepared pieces are glued end to end to form one long length, and success in bending will depend to a large extent upon the bonding of the scarf joints; these should have an inclination of not less than about 1 in 12 and care should be taken to ensure uniform contact of the surfaces to be joined and perfect adhesion. The completed strip is wrapped loosely round a drum or spider from which it may readily be fed on to the bending form. The form may be of wood or metal with a profile of the required shape; a cover plate is fitted to the outer face of the form and extends beyond its perimeter to form a flange, which acts as a guide when the wood is fed on to it.

The form which is mounted on a mechanically driven revolving table, is also provided with a slot into which a wooden block which is glued about 2 inches (50 mm) from one end of the strip can be fitted. When the table is revolved, the form is caused to rotate and the strip is wrapped round it in a spiral form. After a complete turn has been wound on, glue is applied to one face of the strip, usually by means of a glue spreader located at a suitable point along the straight length of strip as it feeds on to the form. Pressure is applied to the glued surfaces

PLATE 15 *Split female form for making hoops*

by means of a tensioned belt which embraces the wood and form in the manner of a band brake, throughout the bending operation. Balata type belting is suitable for this purpose; one end of the belt is anchored securely and it is then passed around the form and the back of the bent strip and tension may be applied by means of a spring-loaded tensioning device, or by a suitable system of weights and levers (*see Plate 16*).

A large variety of continuous-shape types of bend may be made by this method, and obviously non-continuous types may be obtained from these by cross-cutting if desired. Various bends are illustrated in *Plate 17*, and it will be noted that it is possible to produce shapes which include re-entrant curves. In making re-entrant bends, detachable segments are fitted to the form as shown in *Fig. 29*. With these in position during the initial bending operation, it is clear that what will subsequently be the re-entrant portions are first bent in exactly the opposite sense so as to bulge outwards. By this means, the extra length of material required for the re-entrants is obtained, and it is possible before the glue has set, to remove the detachable segments and by means of clamps and male forms to force inwards those parts of the bend previously in contact with these segments, so as to conform to the re-entrant curves desired.

There is a limit, of course, to the variety of shapes that can be produced by this method, and it is impossible to ensure good contact of the wood along straight portions of the form. For this reason all straight portions of appreciable length, where the wood has a natural tendency to belly out, should be held flat during setting by means of boards and cramps.

Laminated inserts

The insert method of producing bent parts is often adopted when the finished wooden member, although straight for the most part, is to contain a curved portion at one or both ends.

The method consists in making longitudinal saw cuts at intervals in the part to be bent, so spaced that the tongues left between the slots are of such a thickness that they are not likely to fracture in the bending operation. Glue-covered laminations cut to the exact length and thickness of the slots are then inserted, (*see Fig. 30*) and the bend made under pressure round the form as already described for the bending of laminated assemblies. It is necessary, of course, to ensure that the thickness of the inserts and of the tongues is such as to permit the bend

to be made without undue difficulty or fracturing. In order to avoid excessive weakening of the sections, the slots should be of varying length so that the ends of the inserts will be staggered.

Two-plane bends

The bending of laminations in the one plane usually presents little difficulty, but the same cannot be said for bending in two planes, and a method such as the following will need to be employed. Laminations, glued and assembled in the normal manner are first bent in one plane to the radius of curvature required. This bend might for instance, take the form of a u having straight legs of sufficient length to provide material for those portions later to be bent in a plane at right angles to the first. The initial bend, after setting, is then sawn normal to the plane of the original laminations into a number of thin curved laminations and glue spread on the surfaces. These are then assembled on the two-plane form, and pressure applied to reunite the central curved portion and to bend and clamp the legs in position. In applying this method, it is obviously necessary to allow, in the initial width of bend, for the wood that is to be removed by the saw cuts, and in this respect the method is somewhat wasteful of material. Appreciable saving of material may be effected by slotting the legs of the initial bend and employing the insert method, described above, for the bend in the other plane.

An alternative method of making the second bend is to treat the initially curved assembly as a solid member. The length to be bent in a plane at right angles to the first one, is steamed in the usual manner and bent without the aid of a supporting strap. This means that the radius of curvature that can be obtained is strictly limited, but it may nevertheless be adequate, if a good bending species is used and only a moderate curvature is required. It is necessary, of course, to use a heat- and water-resistant glue for the initial laminating operation.

Laminated tubes

The continuous-strip method is one that obviously lends itself to the production of laminated cylinders, and examples of cylinders or drums so produced are shown in *Plate 18*. Another method that has been adopted for the manufacture of masts and spars of ships consists essentially of bending across the grain a series of tubes which

Pressing laminations to shape

PLATE 16 *Laminated bending by the continuous strip method*

FIG 29 *Making re-entrant laminated
bends by the continuous strip process*

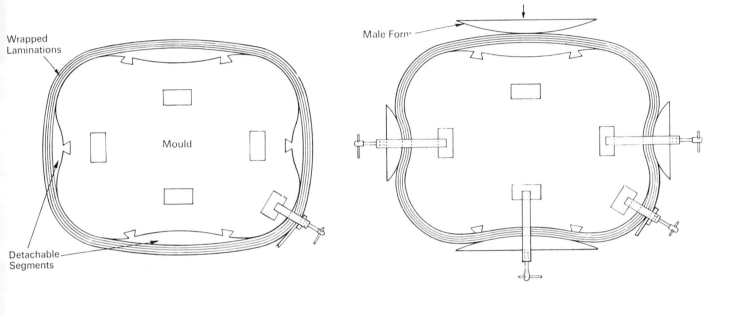

Wrapped
Laminations

Mould

Detachable
Segments

Male Form

PLATE 17 *Various laminated bends
made by the FPRL continuous strip
method*

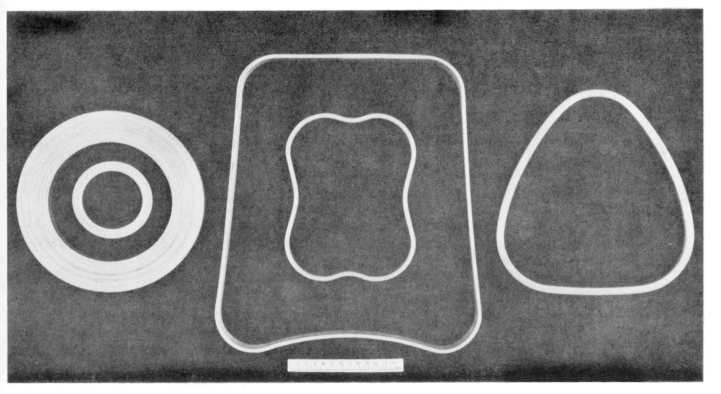

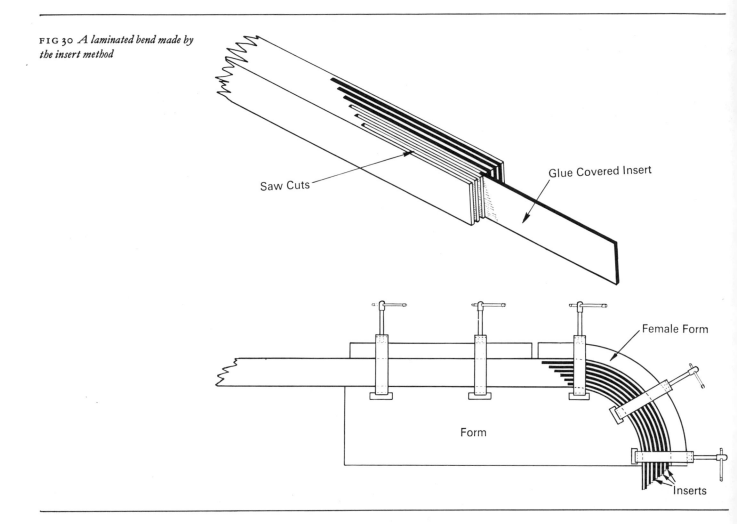

FIG 30 *A laminated bend made by the insert method*

Saw Cuts

Glue Covered Insert

Female Form

Form

Inserts

PLATE 18 *Laminated cylinders made by the continuous strip method*

PLATE 19 *Sections of hollow spars made of Sitka spruce laminations bent across the grain*

fit one over the other to give the required wall thickness, Sitka spruce being the species usually employed. The methods of softening and bending the individual layers have been described previously under the heading 'Prebending'. In the final operation, each concentric tube is scarf-jointed and bonded to the next by the application of glue and radial pressure. In *Plate 19* completed laminated tubes or cylinders so formed are illustrated.

A third method consists of placing a number of preformed laminations, or thin sheets of plywood, inside a metal tube in such a manner that they form concentric and curved layers, the outer one fitting reasonably close to the walls of the metal tube. Just prior to assembling, glue is spread over the surfaces of each layer and, once assembled within the tube, a cylindrically shaped rubber bag is introduced into the space remaining along the axis of the tube. The top and bottom of the tube are tightly sealed and fluid pressure is introduced into the rubber bag, which causes pressure to be exerted radially against the layers of wood. By this means, the concentric layers are pressed tightly one against the other and, once the glue is set, the laminated cylinder is complete. Individual laminations or sheets may be joined by means of scarf, butt, or lap joints according to the final appearance and finish required. An expanding metal or wooden form may sometimes be substituted for the rubber bag and a tightened steel band for the metal tube.

Mention may also be made of the method, described in *British Patent Specification No. 550400*, whereby strips of wood sheeting, veneer or the like are wound helically round a heated metal tube.

Moulding

Unlike certain metals, wood is fissile, and hence not very malleable, so that it cannot easily be moulded or bent in the one operation in two directions at right angles to one another. Some comparatively simple shapes containing compound curvature can indeed be made by pressing veneer sheets between male and female moulds, but if, for instance, it were required that a thin sheet be made to conform to the surface contours of a portion of a sphere of relatively small radius, creases or folds would tend to appear in much the same way as can be seen say from the paper wrapping around a tangerine. In the development of these folds the structural upsets would soon reach a value sufficient to fracture the wood.

To overcome this difficulty and to make possible the production of complex shapes, it is usual to employ veneers which have been tailored or cut so that on applying the pressure necessary to make the wood conform to the shape of the mould, the edges of the cuts come close to one another and form tightly fitting joints or seams. Tailoring, as the name implies, consists essentially, in fashioning or cutting the veneers to fit the mould in much the same way as a tailor would cut cloth for a garment, on the principle that when the pieces have been fitted together and the seams stitched the garment must fit accurately to shape.

In building up consecutive layers of veneers on a mould, one of two methods is normally used. In the first, tailored pieces are assembled one at a time on a mould which is usually of wooden construction. The veneers may take the form of uniform or tapered strips, or sheets from which nicks or slots have been cut depending upon the configuration of the required shape. These are held in place by means of clips or staples, and if cut correctly, the material will fit neatly to shape with butt joints appearing in place of what otherwise would be creases or fractures. When one complete layer has been applied to the mould in this way, glue is spread over the exposed surface, or on the pieces of veneer for the second skin and the next layer is fitted in a similar manner. As the veneers making up each successive layer are applied the staples in the preceding one are removed. Those remaining in the outer layer are finally removed after the adhesive has been cured or set.

A uniform pressure is needed to obtain a good bond, and this is best achieved by means of a rubber sheet or bag and the application of air pressure in the manner previously described under 'Fluid pressure'. In *Plate 20* the process of laying up and clipping glued veneers to form the hull of a boat is illustrated. In this particular type of application, the rubber sheet is placed over the final laminated assembly when the requisite number of layers have been applied; the edges are sealed by clamping to the mould and a vacuum is then drawn. The whole assembly is next wheeled into the autoclave and, as an alternative to air, the autoclave can be filled with live steam under pressure until the adhesive is cured; the hot-moulded hull is then taken out of the autoclave and removed from the mould.

In the second method of making complex shapes, a pre-forming process is used in which the veneer sheet or sheets comprising one layer are tailored and bent roughly to the required shape and edge jointed before actual assembly on the mould. The veneers are often pre-formed by moistening and pressing between male and female dies.

Pressing laminations to shape

PLATE 20 *Laminating veneers in the production of hot-moulded boat hulls*

The butt joints or seams are often 'soldered' together by the application of animal glue, formaldehyde and a hot iron. Strips and pieces forming the outer layer are usually edge-jointed by means of adhesive tape. By feathering the edges, scarf joints may be formed instead of butt joints and layers are often made of two-ply instead of the single veneer.

When the requisite number of sheets or layers has been pre-formed in the above manner, the surfaces are covered with glue and placed one on top of the other over a male form or mould. Fluid pressure may then be applied to the assembly by means of a rubber sheet or bag. When film glue is used, requiring high temperatures and pressures, steam-heated metal male and female moulds are commonly employed.

Setting of the glue

The setting to shape of laminated bends is essentially a process of glue setting, and the method used will therefore depend to a large extent on the type of glue. Other factors, such as the rate of production required, cost, etc., will also need to be considered before any particular method of setting is decided upon. In general, any method which is employed for setting glues in the manufacture of laminated flat assemblies can also be used in bent work.

Most of the older type glues, such as those of the animal or vegetable type, are applied hot, and in most cases it is essential to ensure that the glue has cooled completely before the bend can be removed from the jig without fear of delamination or glue failure. Normally, with glues of this type, the bends remain clamped or pressed to shape overnight, but with special mixes it is sometimes possible to remove them after a period of about three or four hours.

Unlike the glues of the animal and vegetable types, the caseins and synthetic resins become set by virtue of chemical changes taking place in the adhesive, as well as by the loss of moisture, both of which effects can be accelerated by increased temperatures. Heat can be applied to the laminated component in a variety of ways but it is not uncommon to employ low-voltage heating strips for the quick setting of bends of up to, say, one inch in thickness. The steel heating strips carrying a low-tension current of high amperage are joined at one end and placed over the top and bottom surfaces of the bend. They are then connected to a step-down transformer. The temperature aimed at is about 100°C (212°F) and it is

measured by means of a thermo-couple placed close to one of the heating elements. The electrical energy necessary to produce the desired temperature in the strip heater will depend on several variables, such as size, shape and construction of the form, but a power consumption of about 1¾ watts per sq. inch (0·27 watts per cm²) of strip surface area, or approximately ¼ kw. per sq. ft. (2·7 kw. per m²), has been found to be generally satisfactory. For the very quick setting of thicker bends, heating by means of a radio-frequency field might be considered. Metal electrodes here take the place of the heating trips and small holes are bored in the assembly so that thermo-couples can be introduced for temperature readings when the current is turned off and removed when it is switched on again. The temperature should not be allowed to exceed 100°C (212°F) but even so the setting of bends about 2 inches (50 mm) in thickness can, by such means, be accomplished in a period of about 5 minutes.

8 Curved structural laminated members

General considerations

In recent years there has been a considerable increase in production of curved laminated members for structural purposes such as roof arches, top chord truss members, bridges, boat stems, framing, knees and other parts. The advantages and disadvantages of laminating have already been discussed (*Chapter 6*) as they apply to relatively small-dimension members. Some of these also apply where units of structural size are concerned but certain additional factors are of importance. For example in the production of large-section members, the size factor alone rules out the use of solid components in many instances; the size of laminated members continues to increase and depths exceeding 80 inches (2,000 mm) have been used. Strength is always an important consideration and a one-piece curved member sawn from a log would often be inadequate unless made in very large proportions which would then prove to be unacceptable both aesthetically and economically. (The sawing of bent members from large dimension crooks is no longer a practical proposition.)

Where appearance is a primary consideration, as in churches, assembly halls etc., artistic architectural effects, virtually unobtainable with solid timber, can be achieved by using curved laminated members (*see* Plate *21*). Such effects can be further enhanced by a judicious combination of species of different colouring and grain characteristics etc., although for technical reasons care must be exercised in combining different species as is pointed out later.

Apart from being a lengthy operation, the drying of large single-piece members is usually associated with seasoning degrade, and this is largely avoided when using thinner laminations which can be more readily dried before fabrication without checking etc. Another advantage of laminating is that lower-grade material or a weaker species may be used for the less highly stressed laminations. In the construction of highly stressed boat frames for example, the outstanding impact strength combined with the relatively light weight and excellent bending properties of Canadian rock elm are often taken advantage of when this species is used to form the outer laminations of members constructed mainly of African mahogany. In addition, a higher working stress is permissible in laminated construction as a result of a more advantageous dispersion of the defects. The manufacture of an arch with a variable section modulus, or a beam with initial camber for large spans, can also be more easily and effectively achieved when a laminating process is adopted.

Apart from the disadvantages mentioned earlier for small-scale laminating work, an additional factor where structural members are concerned is that the adhesives are often required to possess properties of long-term durability under exposed conditions and such glues are costly; curing techniques are also more critical where glues for exterior situations are used. In the following pages some of the more important aspects to be considered in the production of curved laminated members are briefly discussed, but for full details of the techniques involved in laminating, etc., reference should be made to a manual of 'glulam' construction.

Thickness of laminations

In the fabrication of curved structural members the thickness of the laminations used must obviously be governed also by the radius of curvature to which the pieces may be bent without being damaged. The thicker the material, the fewer the glue lines and the less will be the production cost and loss in sawing, but, tending to offset this are the increased drying costs and mechanical difficulties involved in the bending operation. In general, temperate hardwoods can be bent to a smaller radius of curvature than softwoods, and laminations containing knots and other defects cannot be bent to so small a radius as clear straight-grained material. The values of bending radii already given in *Table 2* relate to $\frac{1}{8}$-inch thick (3·2 mm) laminations, straight-grained and free from all defects, and the radius of curvature given is the one at which not more than one in twenty of the total number of pieces should fracture during bending.

Apart from any limiting radius considerations, the thickness of laminations is generally restricted to 2 inches (50 mm) owing to the difficulty of bending and of drying thicker material without degrade. In addition, the effect on the glue lines of the stresses induced in the timber, resulting from normal moisture content variations and consequent movement in service, is more severe when thicker laminations are used.

There is relatively little information on the radii of curvature to which laminations of different species of structural size may be bent. In practice, it is possible to overstrain the fibres in compression without fracturing the wood. Compression creases which frequently occur before failure of the fibres in tension, impair both the strength and the appearance of a member, and in some instances the latter consideration may be more important than the former. It is known that there is an increase in

PLATE 21 *Curved laminated timber structures*

the ratio of radius of curvature to thickness of lamination $\frac{R}{S}$ with increasing lamination thickness and it is necessary, in arriving at safe working radii for thicker pieces, to apply a factor or factors to the results of laboratory tests on $\frac{1}{8}$ inch (3·2 mm) specimens in order to take this into consideration.

Limited tests made at the Laboratory have indicated that the $\frac{R}{S}$ ratio increases appreciably as the lamination thickness increases from $\frac{1}{8}$ inch to $\frac{1}{2}$ inch (3·2 to 12·7 mm) but thereafter the effect is much less marked. The variation for Baltic redwood (*Pinus sylvestris*) of $\frac{1}{8}$ inch to $\frac{3}{4}$ inch (3·2 to 19 mm) in thickness is shown in *Table 5*. To provide for this thickness effect it would appear that the $\frac{R}{S}$ values derived from tests of $\frac{1}{8}$ inch (3·2 mm) thick material should be increased by a factor of about $\frac{3}{2}$ when thicker laminations are being bent. It is also necessary to take into consideration the limiting curvature reducing effect of knots and defects permissible in the grades of timber used for laminating, although this will be compensated for, to some extent, by bending the laminations in groups rather than individually. In addition, it is not desirable in structural work to assume bending radii equivalent to the radius at failure, since an added margin of safety is required. In the absence of precise data for the species concerned it is suggested that a further factor of $\frac{3}{2}$ should be applied to the $\frac{R}{S}$ ratio (i.e. an overall factor of $\frac{9}{4}$) in deriving a safe value of radius of curvature. The recommended $\frac{R}{S}$ values for structural laminations of a selected number of species bent cold and dry are given in *Table 6*; these values may be taken as a reasonable guide when material up to about 1 inch (25 mm) thickness is being bent. It may be necessary to increase the $\frac{R}{S}$ values somewhat, where low quality material is being used, or where the laminations are substantially above 1 inch (25 mm) in thickness. Conversely lower values may be accepted where straight-grained material, a higher moisture content (which is nevertheless acceptable from the gluing aspect), or thinner laminations are used.

In any curved laminated member the radius of curvature of the inner or concave face will be less than the radius of the outer lamination. Where very deep members are being manufactured this difference may be of such significance as to justify the use of laminations of two thicknesses, with thinner pieces being employed on and near the inner face of the assembly.

Selection and preparation of laminations

In selecting and preparing the laminations similar considerations to those already mentioned for small-scale assemblies apply. Where members are designed to function as structural units, however, such factors as the ability of the material to form a high-strength glue bond, and the strength properties of the species itself frequently assume an even greater importance. Natural durability too may be an important factor in certain situations where there is a decay hazard or risk of insect attack; the moisture content of the laminations and their orientation in respect of direction of the growth rings etc. also become of greater importance as lamination thickness is increased.

(a) *Species and quality*

Although different species vary somewhat in their gluing properties, satisfactory bonding can be obtained with most commercial timbers, even though special care may have to be taken in certain instances, and the 'gluability' of the wood does not usually influence the choice of species.

Hardwoods and softwoods are equally suitable for laminating and the selection of a species for a particular application will depend on such factors as cost and availability as well as durability and stability under changing environmental conditions. Softwoods such as Douglas fir and Western hemlock are commonly used for making large laminated bends because they can be obtained in the required quality and dimensions at a reasonable cost and because they have a relatively high strength-to-weight ratio. In the production of boat timbers on the other hand the severe conditions of service usually demand the use of the more durable hardwoods and oak is the traditional timber for many of the bent members; agba, African mahogany, keruing and other tropical timbers have also been successfully employed, but in some cases the rather poorer bending properties of certain tropical woods necessitates the use of relatively thin laminations.

Natural durability is only an important factor where timbers are in exposed situations, which result in the moisture content attaining a value of 20 per cent or more, but even under these conditions a perishable species pressure-impregnated with a preservative will give every satisfaction from the durability aspect if properly treated. Non-durable sapwood will, of course, respond well to preservative treatment. If the commercially available water-borne preservatives are used, then satisfactory bonding of the laminations can undoubtedly be obtained with resorcinol and phenol-resorcinal type glues provided that special care is taken in the preparation of the pieces to remove any salt deposits, and the correct gluing and curing techniques recommended by the adhesive manufacturers are complied with. The other method of providing protection by pressure impregnation is to treat the completed member rather than the individual laminations; this, however, is virtually impossible where the member is appreciably curved and, in addition, treatment with an aqueous solution under pressure is likely to have undesirable movement and distortional effects on the bend. Where a moderate decay hazard exists, then treatment of the member by brushing, spraying or dipping will probably give the required degree of protection and avoid the troubles associated with a high water absorption.

Laminations which are to be bent to severe curvatures to form highly stressed members generally need to be of straight-grained wood and free of sizeable defects to enable them to be bent to the required shape without fracture occurring. Defects such as large knots and decay patches reduce the effective gluing area, while surfaces containing pitch pockets and resinous areas cannot be glued so effectively as clear wood. Similarly, 'gluability' is reduced when the laminations are prevented from coming into intimate contact by undue amounts of cup, twist, or bow or the presence of proud knots in the board. These defects are permitted in accordance with the strength requirements of the member, and limits are defined in the grading rules for material for glued laminated construction.

(b) *Surface preparation*

Preparation of the timber surfaces is most important in glued laminated work, and planing with cutters correctly set and sharpened is necessary. Where a burnished surface or 'case hardening' has resulted from the use of blunt cutters or from other causes, its removal by sanding or 'toothing' prior to gluing is recommended.

Particular care should be taken to avoid contamination of the prepared surfaces with dust, wax or oil etc. and assembly should be carried out as soon as practicable after planing; the practice adopted by some machine operators of rubbing the table of a planer with paraffin wax to get a smoother feed, is not to be recommended, since it can influence the quality of the glued joint. A time interval of not more than 48 hours between the final preparation of the surfaces and the gluing operation is usually aimed at.

(c) *Moisture content*

In the production of curved members it is very important that the individual laminations are at a suitable moisture content prior to gluing. The required value will be determined by the gluing requirements of the particular adhesive and, within the acceptable range, it should approximate as closely as possible to the average moisture content that the member will attain in service.

In order to produce an efficient glue bond of maximum strength for structural work it is recommended that the timber should have a moisture content of between 7 and 15 per cent. Satisfactory joints for some purposes may, however, be produced from material with values slightly outside this range and an upper limit of 25 per cent is sometimes accepted with resorcinol resin and casein glues.

The timber absorbs moisture from the glue during manufacture of the laminated member and this should be allowed for when considering the equilibrium moisture content that the timber will attain in service. Since moisture content is important, frequent checks should be made on the laminations prior to their preparation for assembly. The electrical resistance type of moisture meter offers a quick and reliable means of doing this, provided that it is regularly calibrated and properly used, and has obvious advantages over the oven-drying method.*

In the United Kingdom there is little likelihood that timber can be dried to below about 20 per cent by air-drying, except for short periods during the year and, hence, kiln drying or some form of artificial drying may be necessary to provide timber that is in a suitable state for glulam construction. In addition, in order to minimize differential shrinkage and swelling in service consequent upon changes in moisture content, and the subsequent development of internal stresses in the member, it is advisable that the moisture content range in an assembly should not exceed 6 per cent. These internal stresses may immediately or eventually lead to failure of the glue bond or checking of the timber.

---

* D. D. Johnston and R. H. Wynands. *A comparison of Readings of a Commercial Resistance-type Moisture Meter and Moisture Contents Determined by Oven-Drying.*

Owing to the difference in movement values of timber in the tangential and radial directions* (a ratio of two to one is not uncommon) material may need to be segregated into quarter-sawn and flat-sawn lots, when species with high movement characteristics are to be used where they are liable to be subjected to appreciable changes in moisture content. Under such conditions it may be advisable not to mix laminations with different growth ring orientation in a single laminated assembly and entirely quarter-sawn laminations are to be preferred. Similarly, when combining two or more species in a member for the sake of appearance, consideration must be paid to the movement values of the species.

Glues

There are generally only three main types of adhesive that need be considered for structural work, namely, casein and the thermosetting resins of the urea and resorcinol type. Although species differ in their gluing properties, satisfactory bonding can be obtained with these adhesives provided the correct techniques have been followed in fabrication, even though special care may need to be taken where certain difficult species such as teak or oak are concerned.

Glues are usually selected on the basis of their durability under the conditions of temperature and humidity to which the structure will be exposed, but other factors such as cost, ease of use in fabrication and curing characteristics etc. may influence the selection. Of these adhesives casein is the most tolerant of conditions in manufacture and the simplest to work; indeed it is a highly versatile adhesive which gives good joints within a considerable range of moisture, temperature and pressure conditions when gluing. It can be set at room temperature, or even at lower than normal temperature, provided that cramping periods are increased accordingly. Although it develops high strength it is, however, only suitable for interior situations, where the mean equilibrium moisture content of the timber will not exceed 18 per cent in use and the temperature will not be higher than about 66°C (150°F).

Urea resins of the room-temperature setting type are used for structural work; they are considerably more moisture resistant than casein, but they are not suitable for use under conditions involving high temperatures and humidities. They are fairly resistant to moisture especially if the temperature is not high, but this is only for limited periods and they cannot be recommended for fully exposed conditions. Their resistance to such conditions can, however, be considerably improved if the urea is combined with melamine or resorcinol resins but such fortified adhesives are more costly and frequently require high curing temperatures. Urea resins are resistant to fungal attack and their light colour may be an advantage; these factors, combined with their relative cheapness and considerable measure of moisture resistance, make them attractive for many applications. The moisture content limits for the timber are rather more critical than for resorcinol resins or casein and to achieve a good bond the upper limit of 15 per cent should not be exceeded.

Resorcinol resin type adhesives are able to withstand the most severe conditions of exposure to heat, humidity and water and, indeed, if the glue joint is properly made, the strength is determined by the ability of the wood itself to resist the exposure conditions. The strength and durability of resorcinol glue bonds are appreciably affected by the curing temperatures. Few set effectively below room temperature and, although for some constructions satisfactory joint strength can be obtained with temperatures of about 20°C (68°F) it has been suggested that for highly-stressed members where the highest quality joint is required, curing temperatures above 60°C (140°F) should be used; this applies especially where dense hardwoods are to be bonded. One disadvantage of resorcinol adhesives is their high cost compared with the other types, but even so, some manufacturers use them exclusively for structural work because of their excellent performance under all conditions. Phenol-resorcinol resins are also available and although highly durable and less expensive than the pure resorcinol types they usually require setting at elevated temperatures.

The cramping times recommended for timber engineering work are usually a minimum of 16 hours or overnight for most applications using normal temperatures but longer periods may be necessary, for example, when resorcinol resin is used to glue oak, for marine work. If elevated temperatures are employed the setting times may be reduced appreciably, and temperatures up to 90–95°C may be used on occasion. The cramping pressures required depend upon various factors such as the type of adhesive, the species of timber, the quality of the laminations and the condition of the surfaces etc. but in general the pressures recommended for structural work are 100 lbf/in² (0·69N/mm²) for softwood and 150 lbf/in² (1·03N/mm²) for hardwoods. These values, however,

---

* *FPRL Leaflet* No. 47

are for straight members; for curved assemblies the cramping pressures will need to be increased appreciably as the lamination thickness is increased and/or the radius of curvature is reduced.

The problem of 'Spring-back' or change in shape of a curved member on release from the form is considered in the following chapter and the effect of lamination thickness is discussed in some detail. In addition to the 'spring-back' reduction that can be achieved by the use of thinner laminations, Freas & Selbo* state that this characteristic feature of bent members can be further reduced by the use of high curing temperatures such as 90°C, maintained for a period of 15 to 20 hours.

In order to estimate the forces necessary to overcome the resistance of the laminations to the bending operation alone and to bring the assembly into contact with the form, it is generally advisable to carry out a 'dry assembly' before any glue is applied to the surfaces. These forces, together with those necessary to produce the required pressures in the glue line, then enable some idea to be obtained of the total forces required in fabricating the member. This information is of use in deciding whether or not the cramping equipment is unduly strained and the operation will demonstrate whether the form etc. is of adequate strength, and the suitability of the cramp spacing to achieve intimate contact of the curved laminations. Although this procedure will give an indication of the cramping forces required, it is always necessary in the actual operation to ensure that the pressures exerted are adequate to maintain the surfaces in intimate contact, and to ensure that the glue forms a thin, uniform and continuous film.

A 'dry run' will also be useful in timing the assembly operation. A carefully planned assembly procedure is required, having regard to the usable life of the glue and attention should be given to the times taken to mix and spread the glue, place the laminations in the correct position, and apply the necessary cramping pressure.

Production techniques

The general underlying principles involved in producing curved structural members are the same as those already outlined in the previous chapter for the making of relatively small wooden bent parts; such differences as

exist being mainly in the techniques involved, and of course, the scale of operations.

Since the forces involved in curving the laminations to shape and applying pressure across the glue lines are often considerable, the forms or jigs must be adequately strong and substantial. It is essential that the cured assembly, when released from its holding clamps, should retain, as far as possible, the curved shape to which it was glued. The form may be constructed for a single curve or may be adjustable to various shapes. A fixed shape may be made of wood or even of metal, but such a construction offers no flexibility and should there be a change of design, calling for a different curvature, new forms would have to be made. In course of time, a wooden form subjected to periodic drying during the setting of the glue, possibly at high temperatures, becomes prone to change shape, if not actually to distort. The fixed form may be mounted either horizontally or vertically depending upon the profile of the required bend.

A common practice is to fabricate forms from a number of brackets made from metal angle plates or sometimes from plywood; these are bolted down to a horizontal perforated or slotted base-plate made of wood or metal (*see Plate 22*). The angles, when not in use, can be freely moved over the face of the frame and then fixed securely in almost any position on it. Initially then, a series of these angle plates would be stationed and secured so as to outline the required profile of the bend. Generally they are located to conform to the concave face (so comprising a male form), though sometimes to that of the convex. In order to provide a smooth and continuous face to the built-up form, a caul or pressure board is first bent round the vertical legs on the metal brackets and secured to them. If the brackets have been located correctly, and allowance has been made for the thickness of the pressure board, then the convex surface of the board will conform to the profile of the inner face of the structural member it is required to produce.

Apart from the permanent cramping bed, various adjustable beds have been developed. One type takes the form of tubular steel trestles which can be screwed into sockets, or bolted to channels, let into the floor; a more convenient working height is achieved by such a method and valuable floor space is not permanently taken up unnecessarily. A variety of methods are available for securing the cramps to the horizontal members of the trestles and two or more members of similar shape may be produced in one operation by cramping the assemblies one above the other. In an alternative method a holding-

---

* A. D. Freas & M. L. Selbo. Fabrication and Design of Glued Laminated Wood Structural Members. *Tech. Bull.* No. 1069. 1954 U.S.D.A.

PLATE 22 *Typical grid-type cramping bed for production of curved laminated members*

down channel is let into the floor and each of the brackets or angles used to make up the form is attached to a long horizontal slotted member which can be bolted down to the channel section. The required profile is achieved by adjusting the position of each slotted member with its attached bracket and bolting down, with an appropriate distance between adjacent members. Whatever the method of cramping adopted, the system must be capable of securing the form and maintaining its shape throughout the cramping and curing period. In setting up a form for a curved assembly it is advisable to carry the line of the form and consequently the length of the laminated assembly well beyond the required final length of the member, especially where there is a sharp curve near the end; failure to do this may lead to distortion.

The assembly of glue-spread laminations is forced to the shape of the form usually by means of screw clamps, but other methods using hydraulic or pneumatically actuated rams or clamping devices with long strokes have been successfully employed. These may result in a very considerable saving in cramping time but, where screw clamps are used, the operation can be speeded up appreciably by using split-nuts and cones developed at the Forest Products Research Laboratory. The cone is simply slipped along the threaded rod and the two hinged halves of the nut are then folded round the thread at the appropriate point and tightened into the cone, thus obviating the necessity of screwing the nut along possibly several inches of the threaded rod. To avoid crushing the wood, and to distribute the pressure evenly, a caul must be inserted between the clamps and the assembly; this may be of metal or more conveniently two or three dummy laminations may be used.

The use of the simple air or water-inflated fire hose frequently used in straight work is not usually employed for curved structural members because of the much greater pressures required, especially with thicker laminations, and the necessity of using some additional clamping equipment to bend the laminations initially into such a position that the deflated fire hoses can become operative between the cauls around the assembly, and a fixed caul secured by the clamping device.

For heavy bends, very considerable forces may be required, and winches or large clamps may be necessary to pull the laminations roughly to shape before actually applying the final clamping pressure. The glue pressures ultimately to be exerted as, already pointed out, must be greater than those recommended by the adhesive manufacturers since the additional force required for the actual bending operation and for the prevention of spring-back must be taken into consideration.

Clamps should not be too widely spaced, and consideration must be given to the force that each one is capable of exerting, the pressure required over the area of the glue-line covered and the force required to hold the laminations to shape. The spacing must be reduced as the bending radius is decreased and for sharply curved members it may be necessary to space the clamps at 6 inches (150 mm) or less apart in order that the required profile is obtained; the proper spacing can best be judged by observing the intimacy of the contact with the form and the behaviour of the laminations as they are clamped in position. The clamping sequence also is important and should be such that the laminations are permitted to slide over each other as the profile is produced. The procedure is to partly tighten all the clamps starting from the centre or from one end of the member, and then to apply full pressure by further tightening in the same sequence. In order to regulate the force applied to a screw clamp it is desirable that the nut should be tightened to the appropriate degree by means of a torque wrench.

Glue setting

For the setting of the glue, any of the methods already referred to may be employed, but structural bends are commonly set by exposing them to air at temperatures above those of the factory conditions. Not only do elevated temperatures speed up the process of setting but they are also necessary in some instances to produce a bond of maximum strength. Where permanent cramping beds are used, steam pipes or other heating units may be located under the base frame. In order to restrict as far as possible hot air to the area to be heated, the assembly may be covered with tarpaulins, rubber blankets, plywood canopies etc.; for less permanent installations, portable electric or oil fan-type heaters may be used to circulate the air through and around the assemblies. Alternatively, when dealing with smaller members, the cramped bend can be taken to a heated chamber for glue setting.

An important factor when applying high temperatures to glued assemblies is the maintenance of an adequate relative humidity. If the air becomes too dry, laminations may dry out and shrink, causing checking of the timber and damage to the glue lines. An appropriate amount of moisture should, therefore, be introduced into the air when setting at high temperatures; this can best be achieved by means of steam or water sprays, used in conjunction with wet and dry bulb thermometers. The relationship between the dry bulb and wet bulb temperatures and consequently relative humidity of the atmosphere and three equilibrium moisture contents of timber are indicated in *Table 7*.

If special equipment of this kind is not available shallow troughs of water may be placed in the heated area and muslin or cloth rags may be hung over the edges to increase the evaporation. With this method little control is possible but, with a certain amount of experience, and by taking periodic checks with a simple hygrometer, reasonable results may be achieved in preventing shrinkage of the timber.

9 The movement and distortion of laminated bends

'Spring-back' of laminated bends

Each lamination in a bent assembly has an inherent tendency to return to its original shape and, but for the bonding of the glue, a bend would proceed to straighten-out as soon as the externally applied forces were removed. On removing a laminated bend from a form, some outward movement does, in fact, tend to occur, and shear stresses are induced in the glue lines. Movement continues until the induced moment of resistance in the piece just balances the residual bending moments in the laminations. Shear forces in the glue tend to be greater near the ends than at the centre of a bend, and movements leading to straightening are therefore always more permanent near the ends*.

The extent of these outward movements or the radius increase usually referred to as 'spring-back' has been investigated at the Laboratory. From theoretical considerations the following formula has been evolved which gives a measure of the spring-back that has been found to correspond reasonably well with that found in practice†.

The percentage radius change (spring-back) is given as $100 \left(\dfrac{1}{n^2 - 1} \right)$ where n equals the number of laminations in the bend. From this it will be seen that when only two laminations are used, the percentage spring-back likely to occur would be of the order of $33\frac{1}{3}$ per cent, whereas, by increasing the number of laminations to five, the percentage spring-back is reduced to not much more than 4 per cent of the initial radius of the form. In practice, the effect of such movements can often become masked by movements or changes in radius of curvature brought about by moisture changes.

Movement of bends

Loss or gain of moisture in a piece of bent wood will cause both its width and thickness to alter, but will not materially affect the longitudinal dimensions unless considerable compression has occurred in this direction. In laminated bends, longitudinal compressive strains are generally comparatively small, and the laminations behave, as far as dimensional changes due to moisture are concerned, in much the same way as in the unbent state. When drying takes place in a bend that is set there is a

tendency for the inner and outer surfaces to come closer together without any appreciable change occurring in the peripheral lengths of these surfaces. It is reasonable to suppose, that in set laminated bends, initially plane cross-sections of the piece tend to remain plane for relatively small moisture changes, in which case it becomes necessary for the radius of curvature of the bend to alter in order that the piece as a whole should conform to the dimensional changes that have occurred. Suppose the original thickness of a bend made to a form radius r to be t and that this shrinks by an amount e per unit of thickness so that the final thickness of bend is $t(1-e)$. The peripheral lengths l_1 and l_2 of the inner and outer surfaces, respectively, remain virtually unchanged so that, if the assumption that plane sections remain plane is valid, then the following relation holds:

$$\frac{l_1}{r_1} = \frac{l_2}{r_1 + t(1-e)}$$

where r_1 is the new radius of curvature.

$$\text{but } l_1 = \frac{l_2 r}{r + t}$$

$$\text{So that } \frac{r}{r_1(r + t)} = \frac{1}{r_1 + t(1-e)}$$

Hence $rr_1 + rt(1-e) = rr_1 + r_1 t$

or $r_1 = r(1-e)$.

This result is of interest as it indicates that the percentage decreases in radius of curvature should be exactly equal to the percentage decrease in the thickness of the bend caused by moisture loss, a result borne out by test.

Similarly, it can be shown that the unit increase in the angle of bend expressed in radians should be equal to $\dfrac{e}{1-e}$. Much the same reasoning may be applied to solid bends, except that here the movements are augmented by the fact that compressed wood tends to expand and shrink in the longitudinal direction with moisture gain and loss, and for this reason such bends are usually less stable than similar bends of laminated type. Finally, it follows that in both cases bends made from quartered material tend to move rather more than bends made from plain-sawn (slash-cut) material.

Other things being equal, the thinner the laminations the less the tendency for a set bend to open on release of the pressure but, unfortunately, the thinner the laminations the greater the quantity of glue used.

---

* W. W. Barkas. Tangential and Radial Stresses in Two-ply Circular Bends. *F.P.R.L. Unpublished Report*, August 1945.

† W. C. Stevens, m.a., a.m.i.mech.e. and N. Turner. *Wood*, Vol. 22, pp. 44–48, February 1957.

All glues normally used for bent work contain moisture in varying amounts, which naturally tends to find its way into the wood and so raise its moisture content. Since setting usually occurs before all this moisture is removed, the bend tends subsequently to dry out in the workshop or in service, with consequent reduction in the radius of curvature.

Ideally, therefore, the amount of moisture added by the glue, and the consequent inward movement caused by its removal, should be just enough to compensate for the initial outward movement referred to above.

In actual practice, however, control of this process is virtually impossible, and where accuracy of shape is of paramount importance it is advisable to use a glue containing as little moisture as possible. The minimum quantity consistent with strength should be used, and the laminations conditioned initially to a moisture content corresponding to conditions of service. Solely from this aspect, glue types may be graded as follows:

Phenol-formaldehyde,

Urea-formaldehyde,

Casein,

Animal.

Naturally, in the selection of any glue for a specific purpose, other aspects such as strength, resistance to moisture, cost, etc., need to be taken into consideration.

Distortion of bends

In the bending of any elastic material, compression and tensile stresses are induced along the concave and convex surfaces respectively. These direct stresses tend always to produce strains in their own direction, but at the same time to produce opposite kinds of strain in perpendicular directions. Thus the longitudinal shortening of the compressed concave surface is accompanied by a lateral expansion, and similarly the longitudinal stretch of the convex surface is accompanied by a lateral shortening. It thus follows that by bending the material in one plane a tendency will be induced for it to bend in a plane at right angles to the first but in the opposite sense.

Curvature which results from bending moments so induced appears in the form of cupping of the cross-section of a bent piece, but usually the extent of the distortion so produced is small and of little consequence.

Curved or flat laminated assemblies containing grain that deviates from the straight are, however, subject to distortion as the result of moisture change in much the same way as boards of solid timber. If wood with curved grain is used there will be a tendency, when drying occurs, for the piece as a whole to curve in the same direction as the curvature of the grain. Similarly, if the grain is spiral there will be a tendency for the assembly to twist in drying. Troubles from such causes obviously can be eliminated by selecting only straight-grained material for the work and, above all, by ensuring that all pieces are conditioned to the same moisture content before assembly.

Even with the use of straight-grained material, however, curvature of the cross-section, usually referred to as cupping, may occur unless the material is properly quartered. Plain-sawn laminations assembled so that the annual rings, as they appear on the ends, are more or less concentric, will curve or cup on drying in a direction opposite to that of the ring curvature.

Still more marked would be the effect if the top half of an assembly consisted of plain-sawn material and the bottom half of quarter-sawn, since stresses would be set up across the section and glue lines as a result of excess shrinkage or expansion of the plain-sawn over the quartered material, leading to curvature of the section. It is possible to minimize such effects by assembling individual laminations in a balanced manner such as that shown in *Fig. 31*, so that the tendency of any pair to curve in one direction is offset by a like tendency for another pair to curve in the opposite direction. As, however, stresses in the glue lines are thereby induced this method cannot be generally recommended. Moreover, it must be realized that, in applying such methods, the balance of stress so achieved may be upset by subsequent machining of the parts.

Straightness of grain does not preclude the possibility of the laminated assembly twisting as a result of moisture change unless the grain is absolutely parallel with the sides, or parallel grain exists throughout the assembly. To illustrate the effect that inclination of grain may have upon the twisting of laminated bends, *Fig. 32* is drawn to represent an assembly made of two laminations with the grain of the top piece inclined at an angle to the grain of the bottom. The diagonal lines represent grain lines as they appeared before assembly on the top and bottom pieces. The inclination of the grain to the sides of each lamination is assumed here to be the same.

If now it is assumed that virtually no shrinkage takes place in the direction of the grain but that there is shrinkage in the direction normal to the grain as a result of drying, it is apparent that the top right-hand corner x and bottom left-hand corner y of the top lamination will

FIG 31 *End view of laminated assembly with annual rings so arranged as to counteract cupping tendency*

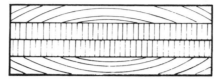

FIG 32 *Diamonding effect leading to twist*

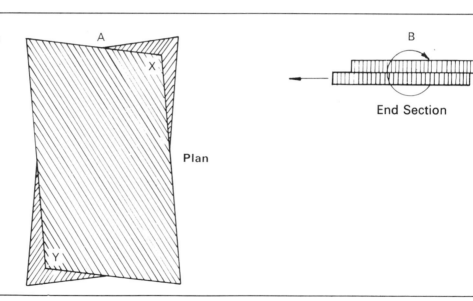

A

X

Plan

Y

B

End Section

FIG 33 *End view of laminated assembly with annual rings arranged in herringbone pattern*

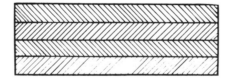

tend to approach one another, and the other two corners will also tend to approach one another, but to a much less extent. The face of the lamination will in effect diamond, and the longer edges tend to orientate themselves in the direction of the grain. The lower lamination will behave similarly, but the orientation will be in the opposite direction.

If they were to move, the end sections would assume relative positions as illustrated diagrammatically in *Fig. 32*. The glue, however, inhibits the relative movement, and consequently forces are developed, with the top lamination pulling in one direction with a force P, and the bottom in the other direction with an equal force P. These two forces form a couple or turning moment which tends to twist one end in an anti-clockwise direction and the other in a clock-wise direction as viewed from either end. The whole piece is thus subjected to torsion, and twisting is the probable outcome.

It follows that by crossing the grain of two or more laminations in a pack, a tendency for the glued assembly to twist is induced as a result of subsequent moisture change. The intensity of twisting likely to develop will be dependent upon a number of factors, such as degree of moisture change, the angle of crossing of the grain lines, the relative positions and thicknesses of the parts having opposed grain, strength characteristics, etc.

It has been suggested that twist may be minimized by assembling the laminations so that the annual rings on the end cross-section form a herringbone pattern (*see Fig. 33*). Tests have shown, however, that this method of assembly has little if any control upon subsequent twisting, which fact is illustrated by the bends shown in *Plate 23*. Here the bend on the left was made from an assembly of laminations having grain at an angle to the sides but parallel throughout and with the annual rings on the end section sloping in one direction. The bend on the right was made from matched material, but assembled so that the grain of the lamination on the concave face was sloping in the opposite direction to the remainder. The annual rings on the end section of this particular bend were in perfect herringbone formation, yet, as may be observed, the twist that subsequently developed was very pronounced. Hence the herringbone assembly method can be recommended only in so far as it tends to minimize subsequent cupping of the cross-section of a piece.

The best method of avoiding twisting troubles would seem to be to select perfectly straight-grained material having the grain absolutely parallel with the length of piece. Failing this, however, it is recommended that the greatest care should be taken to ensure that the grain of the several laminations in a pack is parallel throughout, which requirement can best be fulfilled by assembling the packs from laminations in the order cut. Twisting may also, of course, be minimized or eliminated by arranging that any pair of laminations with crossed grain, which would tend to twist the assembled bend, say, to the right, is counterbalanced by another pair tending to twist it with an equal force to the left. Such balancing is not easy to accomplish in practice and is not to be recommended as a general method of procedure. Finally, if none of the above methods proves feasible, it remains to ensure so far as possible that the moisture content of the bent pieces does not alter after setting, so that no shrinkage or swelling occurs up to the time that they are incorporated in the finished product. Bends already twisted may, of course, be similarly made serviceable by conditioning back to their original moisture value, but it must be borne in mind that when subsequent moisture changes occur in service, such conditioned bends may cause trouble by twisting out of shape and possibly producing distortions in the finished article in which they are incorporated. `

PLATE 23 *The twisting of laminated bends*

Left: Bend assembled with the grain of all laminations parallel and annual rings on end section sloping in one direction

Right: Bend assembled with the grain of one lamination on the concave face sloping in the opposite direction to remainder and with the annual rings forming herringbone pattern on end section

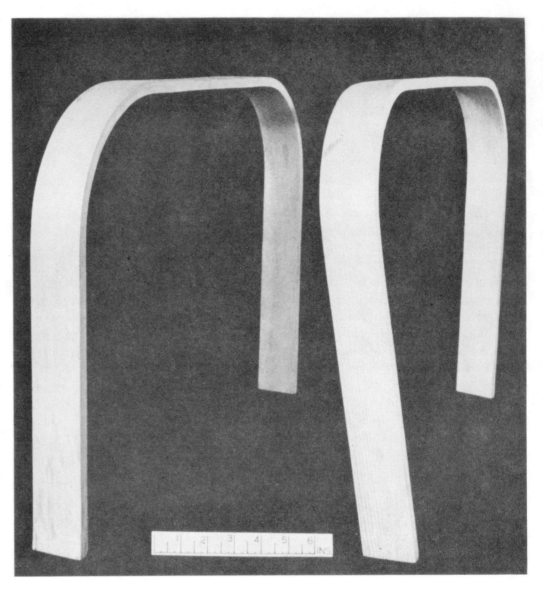

Part C: Plywood bending

10 *Factors affecting the bending of plywood*

General considerations

Curved shapes, made by taking flat sheets of commercial plywood and bending them to the required profile round suitable forms or moulds, have many uses in the production of chair parts, travel goods, radio and television cabinets, containers and the like (*Plate 24*). Although plywood bends of this sort have rather less rigidity and in conditions of changing atmospheric humidity tend to be somewhat less stable than similar bends made by gluing a pack of veneers and pressing them to shape, nevertheless, for purposes such as those already mentioned and where the plywood bend is held to shape by, say, the rest of the structure of which it forms a part, shapes produced in this way are quite serviceable and usually less costly to make than comparable laminated bends.

The manufacture of flat plywood consists essentially of gluing together in a suitable press a number of veneers or plies arranged so that the grain directions of successive layers are at right angles to each other. Once this has been done, no further movement of the plies relative to one another can take place without a breakdown of the glue bond and the destruction of the plywood as such.

In forming a curved shape from this sort of material it is clear that the difference in length between the convex and concave faces of the bend cannot be brought about by the plies or veneers sliding over one another as in laminated bending but must result from tensile and compressive strains induced in the material by the bending operation. The radius of curvature required and the thickness of the plywood to be bent will affect the difference in length between the convex and the concave faces of the bend and, hence, the magnitude of the strains which have to be induced, whereas the ability of the material to conform to the strains imposed will be affected by such factors as the species of timber and its moisture content, the grain direction of the face plies and any softening treatment that has been used.

Owing to the practical difficulties involved in the use of a metal strap for the control of fibre movements when bending a comparatively thin sheet material such as plywood, in most cases the strap is dispensed with altogether and the material is bent in the unsupported state. Hence, as the radius of curvature of the plywood bend is decreased, tension stresses build up in the ply on the convex face of the bend until eventually the breaking point is reached and tension failure occurs. The ability of this ply to withstand the stresses imposed will, of course, be reduced by the presence of knots, splits, checks, inclined grain and so on, and it is important,

therefore, to select as clear a face as possible for what is to become the convex face of the finished bend. Any gaps or voids in the cross banding or intermediate plies in the area of the bend should also be avoided if possible, as they may well bring about a premature failure of the bend by causing local increases in curvature.

Factors affecting plywood bending

When considering the bending of a piece of plywood, one of the most important items of information required is the smallest or limiting radius of curvature that can be attained before the tension face of the bend is stretched to breaking point. Some of the factors that affect this radius are as follows:

(a) *Species*

The influence of species on the limiting radii has been determined by standard tests and the results obtained are indicated diagrammatically in *Fig. 34*. They indicate the range of limiting radii of curvature likely to be encountered with $\frac{3}{16}$ inch (4·8 mm) plywood bent cold and along the grain at a moisture content of 10 per cent. In general, plywood made from the temperate-grown hardwoods appears to possess better bending properties than that from softwoods and tropical hardwoods. No hard and fast rules can be laid down however and it is advisable for preliminary practical tests to be made in all cases.

(b) *Thickness of specimen*

Since the limiting radius of curvature for any species of plywood is dependent upon the strains which can be induced in the face veneers before breakage occurs, and because these limiting strains would depend upon the particular species used, it might be expected that a change in thickness of the plywood would result in a proportional change in limiting radius of curvature and that the ratio of limiting radius to thickness would remain constant.

Experiments have indicated that this is not so, however, and as with solid wood laminations, (*Chapter 8*) the ratio of radius of curvature to thickness of plywood tends to increase when the thickness of the specimen being bent is increased. This effect can be seen from *Table 8* where the results of tests upon a range of thicknesses of African mahogany and Finnish birch plywoods are given. The results appear to show that the percentage strain that can be induced in bending a thick specimen is less than can be induced when bending a thin one.

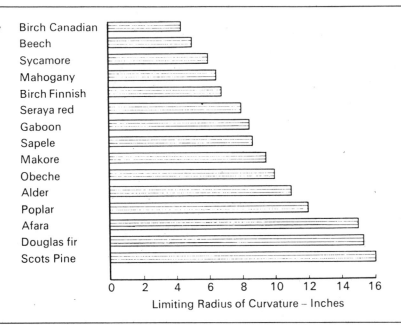

FIG 34 *Limiting radii of curvature for plywood species*

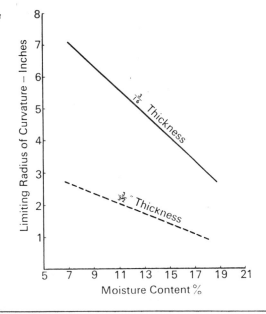

FIG 35 *Effect of moisture content on the limiting radius of curvature of African mahogany 3-ply bent cold and along the grain*

PLATE 24 *Some examples of plywood bends used in industry*

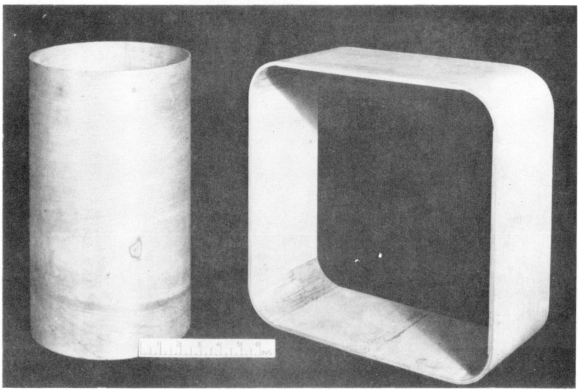

(c) *Grain direction of the face plies*

Since plywood is manufactured as a sheet material it is just as likely to be bent across the grain (i.e. with the grain of the face veneer parallel to the axis of the bending form) as it is to be bent along the grain (with the grain of the face veneers perpendicular to the axis of the form). The extent to which timber can be compressed and stretched across the grain is quite different from that which it will tolerate along the grain and different limiting radii of curvature values are obtained. Timber can generally be strained more easily and to a greater extent across than along the grain and plywood bent across the grain is found to bend to smaller radii of curvature than when bent along it. This is particularly true of three-ply material where the ratio of material bent across the grain to material bent along it is 2:1 and the radii of curvature obtained are as low as 0·5 or 0·6 of those of comparable material bent along the grain. As the number of plies is increased, however, to, say, 7 the ratio of material bent across the grain to that bent along it is reduced to 1⅓:1 and the radii of curvature for across grain bending are as high as 0·9–0·95 of those of comparable material bent along the grain. When bent in comparatively narrow strips 1–2 inches (25–50 mm) wide, plywood with the face grain at an angle of 45° to the length of the specimen has a limiting radius of curvature lying between those of the material bent in the other two grain directions. It must be noted, however, that particularly in the case of three-ply material, the relative ease with which the plies can be bent across the grain results in a tendency for the 45° specimens to take up a helical path round the form and, in addition to the force required to make the bend, other forces have to be applied in a direction parallel to the axis of the form to counteract this. When wider specimens are being bent, there is a tendency for the cross-section of the specimen to become slightly dished, with its edges lifting somewhat away from the bending form and for a number of small surface checks to develop.

(d) *Moisture content*

Changes in moisture content below fibre-saturation point alter the mechanical properties of timber and, in the case of plywood, affect its limiting radius of curvature by modifying the force required and the extent to which the individual plies can be compressed or stretched during the bending operation. The results of tests carried out at the Forest Products Research Laboratory on the bending of African mahogany plywood (*Fig. 35*) show that an increase of about 11 per cent in its moisture content reduces the limiting radius of curvature to a value just over one-third of that at the higher moisture content. This should be borne in mind when the moisture content of plywood for bending is being considered as also should be the desirability of some form of moisture content control of the material if consistently good bends are to be produced.

(e) *Temperature*

When thin plywood is being bent, heat applied to the concave face during the bending operation by means of heated forms appears to have some softening or plasticising effect and allows smaller radii of curvature to be attained. Tests on 4 mm ($\frac{5}{32}$ inch) Finnish birch show that a limiting radius of 8¾ inch (222 mm) on a cold form can be lowered to one of 7½ inch (190 mm) if the surface temperature of the form is increased to 176°C (350°F). On material of thicknesses much greater than this, however, the method largely becomes ineffective and no worthwhile advantage can be gained from its use.

I I *Production of plywood bends*

Softening processes

If the amount of curvature required cannot be obtained by means of the heating technique indicated in the previous chapter, then additional fibre movement and hence smaller radii of curvature can be obtained by use of a softening treatment before bending. This consists essentially of exposing the plywood to be bent to the action of moisture or, more usually, to both heat and moisture. The treatments commonly used range from dipping the plywood in cold water to boiling or steaming it long enough to heat it throughout its thickness.

The latter treatments are, of course, more effective, but care must be taken to ensure that the glue used in manufacturing the plywood will withstand these conditions. For example, when boiling or steaming methods are to be employed, plywood with a WBP or a BR* glue bond is essential. For plywood with an MR* glue bond, immersion in water at 67°C (152°F) for the length of time usually required to soften it should not involve very much risk of delamination, but for plywood not falling in these categories often the best that can be done is to use a one-second dip in boiling water.

Although dip treatments cannot be expected to fully soften plywood for bending, it can be well worthwhile for thin material. For example, using $\frac{3}{16}$ inch (4·8 mm) African mahogany three-ply, a one-second dip in cold water reduces the limiting radius of curvature to about three-quarters of that of untreated material, but if boiling water is substituted, the corresponding figure is reduced to one half the radius obtainable with dry plywood. It is to be expected, however, that the efficacy of dip treatments will decrease as the thickness of the plywood is increased.

The smallest radii of curvature are obtained when the specimen is immersed in boiling water. The recommended treatment time is 2 minutes per millimetre thickness which is approximately 10 minutes for $\frac{3}{16}$ inch (4·8 mm) plywood. This is appreciably longer than the time taken for heat to penetrate to the centre of the specimen, for tests show that this takes place in about 2 minutes; nevertheless, throughout the period the specimen is absorbing moisture and this must also play a part in softening or plasticising the material. Substantial lowering of limiting radii of curvature can be achieved by treatments such as this and reductions of the order of 5:1 are not uncommon. With softening treatments using water at 67°C (152°F), results very nearly as good can be obtained, but at the expense of doubling the treatment time.

Although equally good results in terms of small limiting radii of curvature can be obtained by exposing the specimens to saturated steam at atmospheric pressure, this medium is found to be a less effective wetting agent than boiling water and it is thought that this is the reason why treatment times tend to become prolonged – in excess of 30 minutes for $\frac{3}{16}$ inch (4·8 mm) thick plywood.

The species and the grain direction of the face plies are factors which also affect the limiting radius of curvature of plywood in the softened state. The standard test procedure at the Forest Products Research Laboratory provides data, where possible, on material $\frac{3}{16}$ inch (4·8 mm) thick bent in the fully softened (boiled) state as well as when bent cold, and includes both material bent along and across the grain. Over the years a considerable body of information has been built up and the findings for a number of the better known plywoods are shown in *Table 9*.

Methods of bending

In many cases such as shopfitting, boat building and the like, where shaped joinery has been fitted up or a profiled framework of ribs and stringers is available, it is often merely a matter of forcing the plywood strips or sheets to the required shape by hand pressure or by means of simple clamps and securing them to the framework by screwing, pinning and gluing, or any other convenient means. Where this procedure is inappropriate, however, as for example when a plywood bend is required as a component of a typewriter case, then hand- or power-operated machinery has to be employed.

Although there are one or two machines of American origin available in this country, there is at the present time a shortage of British-made machines designed solely for the production of bent plywood so that many manufacturers make for themselves the equipment required for their particular job on hand. The essentials comprise a suitably shaped form, a means of clamping the plywood specimen to it and a means of wrapping the plywood sheet closely round the form. These forms are usually heated and if they are made of metal, mains voltage electric heaters can be incorporated, but if made of multi-ply wood, as is often the case, then low voltage strip heating can be employed. Mechanical or pneumatically-operated clamping bars are used to secure the plywood to the form and the actual shaping may be done by a suitably shaped female form or by rotating the form and employing a pneumatic pressure roller to keep the plywood

---

* B.S. 1203:1954 – Synthetic Resin Adhesives for Plywood.

specimen closely in contact with it. The modification of a vertical revolving table into a machine for bending test specimens of plywood is shown in *Plate 25*. The metal form is of $1\frac{1}{2}$ inch (38 mm) radius and is heated to 150°C (300°F).

The $\frac{3}{16}$ inch-thick (4·8 mm) African mahogany plywood shown being bent was previously softened by boiling, and is held in position at the start of the bend by means of the pneumatically-operated clamping bar. The pressure roller moves in guides positioned so that the force is applied radially with respect to the bending form. When using a pressure roller with a material as thin as this, there is sometimes a tendency for the specimen to bend backwards away from the form just before it comes into contact with the pressure roller. This can, however, be overcome by feeding the plywood on to the roller by means of a backplate about 2 inch (50 mm) wide, the surface of which is tangential to the roller's surface at the point of bending the plywood.

The speed of bending should not be too great, for it has been found that the percentage of breakages tends to increase at high rates of bending. On the other hand, there is nothing to be gained by bending too slowly and tests have indicated that a bending speed of about 6 revs/min is a good working compromise.

The forces involved in bending will, of course, depend to a large extent on the thickness, width and species of the plywood being bent. In general they are not high, for with a material of cross-banded construction such as this, some part of the specimen is bound to be bent across the grain and for this only a comparatively small force will be needed. The 2 inch (50 mm) diameter air rams illustrated working at an airline pressure of 80–100 lbf/in² (0·55–0·69N/mm²), are, in fact, capable of dealing with African mahogany plywood (softened by boiling) up to $\frac{3}{8}$ inch (10 mm) thick and 6 inch (150 mm) wide. The torques required to rotate the form are, again, not excessive and a 1 hp (750 watt) motor, suitably geared down, should enable a large variety of material to be dealt with. In one make of imported bending machine* the motor is dispensed with entirely and the form is rotated by means of a system of levers and weights.

In yet another make of imported machine† no rotating parts are used at all. A subsidiary pneumatic clamping

system secures what is to become the apex of the bend to the heated form, the surface of which is often fluted or splined, and the main air cylinders then actuate suitably shaped female forms to force the plywood to the required shape.

Setting of plywood bends

In bending plywood to a curved shape, longitudinal compressive and tensile strains are induced in both concave and convex faces and latent stresses remain in the material when the bending operation is completed. If at the end of the process the clamping bars, pressure rollers, and the like were to be removed immediately, then these stresses would cause the plywood to open out and return nearly to the straight. To enable plywood to retain its curved shape, therefore, it is necessary either to reduce the magnitude of these latent stresses, or increase the overall stiffness of the bend, or possibly employ a combination of the two. Whatever the precise mechanism may be, it is clear however, that setting can be accomplished, as with a solid bend, by the removal of moisture and that this can be accelerated by the application of heat. In the case of plywood bends, the most usual way to achieve this is to heat the surface of the form on which the bend is to be made. Because of the comparative thinness of the material, heat is quickly conducted through its mass and much of the contained moisture is rapidly driven off.

In considering the setting of plywood bends, the actual form temperature is an important factor and to a large extent determines the treatment time that is required. The results of a number of tests, using mostly $\frac{3}{16}$ inch (4·8 mm) thick African mahogany, showed that to obtain the same amount of set as is achieved in 5 minutes' treatment when the surface temperature of the form is 150°C (300°F), it is necessary to leave the bend clamped to the form for 20 minutes when its surface temperature is reduced to 100°C (212°F). Care must be taken, however, when using temperatures appreciably above boiling point, for there is always a risk that the concave face of the bend in contact with the source of heat will become darkened in colour to some extent. Although this effect is not so noticeable with the dark-coloured mahogany plywood, with lighter-coloured species such as beech or birch it cannot be ruled out and, for these timbers, a lower temperature treatment for a longer time may prove to be preferable. The use of temperatures above 150°C (300°F) does not appreciably shorten the setting time and the risk

---

* The Ladon Bending Machine, Midwest Manufacturing Co., St. Louis, U.S.A.

† The Handy Bending Press, Handy Manufacturing Co., Chicago 25 U.S.A.

PLATE 25 *An experimental plywood bending machine*

of discolouring or scorching the concave face of the bend is, of course, increased.

The thickness of the plywood from which the bend is made does not appear to have so great an effect on the setting time as might at first be supposed, though the times obtained experimentally by bending various thicknesses of plywood over the same form may have been, to some extent, affected by the changing ratio of radius of curvature to thickness. The net effect, however, seems to be that a setting time of about 5 minutes on a form whose surface temperature is 150°C (300°F) is suitable for plywood thickness from $\frac{3}{64}$ inch to $\frac{3}{16}$ inch (1·2 to 4·8 mm) whereas for $\frac{3}{8}$ inch (9·5 mm) thick material the best results are obtained when the time is increased by 50 per cent to $7\frac{1}{2}$ mins.

By choosing the appropriate values of treatment time and form temperature, it is possible to set a plywood bend so that when taken from the bending form and measured, it has exactly the same inside diameter as the form on which it was made. However, the shape of the bend immediately off the form is not the best criterion to adopt when assessing the accuracy of set of the bend and it is generally considered to be preferable to let it come into equilibrium with its surroundings (at, say, 10 per cent moisture content) and then measure its diameter, for it is in this condition that it will eventually be used. The best that can be expected is that the set bend will reach stability with its diameter about 5 per cent greater than the diameter of the form on which it was made. Any attempt to improve on this figure by prolonging the setting time or using higher form temperature merely overdries the bend and resultant moisture pick-up causes it to open out more than before, even though when first removed from the form the bend may spring inwards to a sharper curvature than that to which it was originally bent.

Other factors affecting the accuracy of set of plywood bends include the ratio of radius of curvature to thickness of the bend, the grain direction of the face plies and the softening treatment, if any, to which the material may have been subjected. When plywood of various thicknesses, first softened in boiling water, is bent over a form of given radius, it is found that thicker material can be set to a more accurate shape than the thinner and alternatively if plywood of constant thickness is bent on forms of decreasing radii, the best set is obtained with bends made on the smallest radii forms. In other words, the most accurate set is obtained, other things being equal, when the ratio of radius of curvature to thickness is low;

i.e. when high strains have been induced in the specimen in making the bend.

Plywood bent across the grain (with the grain of its face layers parallel to the axis of the bending form) is also difficult to set accurately to shape. Because the majority of the plies or veneers are being bent in their weakest direction, the finished bend is inherently less stiff than a comparable piece of plywood bent along the grain and, hence, tends to move out on release from the form. Furthermore, whilst the concave face of the bend, which has been in contact with the hot surface of the form, is coming back into moisture content equilibrium with the atmosphere, the whole of its lateral expansion is acting circumferentially around the concave face of the bend to reduce its curvature. As a result, the outward movements commonly found in bends of this sort are a good deal greater than those of comparable material bent along the grain. It may be pointed out, however, that if the cross grain bend is to be incorporated into an assembly, then the lack of stiffness mentioned above makes it comparatively easy to spring it into position. Plywood bent with its face grain at an angle of 45° to its length behaves in a manner intermediate between these two extremes, but it frequently develops a certain amount of twist and in some cases the concave face is found to be somewhat dished in a direction parallel to the axis of the bend.

Plywood which has been softened or plasticized before bending appears to set better to shape than material which has only undergone a dip treatment or has been bent dry. The results of tests on $\frac{3}{16}$ inch (4·8 mm) mahogany plywood show that only marginal differences in subsequent behaviour exist between bends made from material which has been boiled first and that which has been immersed in water at 67°C (152°F) to soften it. On the other hand, bends made from plywood which has only been dipped in boiling water move outwards twice as much as those made from fully softened material. No systematic tests have been carried out on the setting of plywood bends in the dry state, but preliminary indications are that the outward movements here would be even greater than those of the dipped material.

In some cases it may be possible to remove the finished bend from the form immediately it is made and it can then be held across the ends in suitable clips and put to set in a conventional setting room heated to, say, 65°C (150°F) dry heat. If this is done, then setting times of the order of 30 minutes for $\frac{3}{16}$ inch (4·8 mm) thick plywood can be adequate. With a suitable setting room or even a large electric oven, the output of a given bending machine might be increased, but of course only comparatively simple circular shapes can be taken off the form in this way and care is needed to avoid any excessive outward movement when removing the bend from the form for distortion of the shape is almost bound to occur if it has to be forced into the retaining clips.

Change in shape of bends

When a plywood bend has been set to shape it must not be thought that no further changes in curvature are possible. Plywood bent along the grain is rather like a solid bend in so far as in each case longitudinal compressive strains have been induced in the material on the concave face of the bend during the shaping process, and this compressed material will tend to shrink and expand longitudinally with changes in atmospheric humidity, thereby altering the curvature of the bend.

Thus a plywood bend of this sort will open out and increase its radius of curvature if exposed to air of a higher humidity and will close up and decrease its curvature when exposed to a lower humidity. If these changes in humidity, and hence the changes in the moisture content of the bend are kept reasonably small, then the resulting movements, although larger than for a comparable laminated bend, will be small and to all intents and purposes reversible. If, on the other hand, the moisture content of the bend is allowed to rise too high (in the range 18–20 per cent), then large outward movements take place and these cannot be reversed completely by redrying the bend. This effect is more marked with thin plywoods of, say, $\frac{3}{32}$ inch (2·4 mm) thickness than with the thicker ones ($\frac{3}{8}$ inch (10 mm)), and is less marked with severe bends than with simple shapes with a high ratio of radius of curvature to thickness.

The above remarks apply, of course, to free-standing plywood bends with unrestricted movement. It is, however, unlikely that this tendency of a plywood bend to change in shape with changes in atmospheric humidity will materially affect its usefulness as a component part of any larger article where the rest of the structure will hold the bend firmly to shape.

Bent corners

In the production of radio and television cabinets, some articles of furniture and the like, it is often necessary to bend thick plywood, say 9 mm and above, to radii of curvature of 1 inch (25 mm) or even less to form what may perhaps be best described as rounded corners. It is obvious that none of the techniques described above will provide bends of this severity and other methods which involve machining away (instead of compressing) the surplus material on the concave face of the bend will have to be employed.

(a) *The saw kerf corner*

Saw kerfing is a method often used, and this consists of cutting a series of slots in what is to be the concave face of the bend by means of multiple saws mounted on a single spindle. The slots are cut straight across the piece to be bent in a direction parallel to the axis of the bending form and in depth extending to within two plies of the opposite face. If the plywood has a decorative veneer glued to it, then this is counted as one of the plies. The amount of material to be removed circumferentially will depend on the thickness of the plywood and the radius of curvature of the required bend and it is usually arranged so that the slots on the concave face are on the point of closing as the bend is completed (*see Plate 26*). To obtain the best curve on the convex face, the slots must not be too widely spaced and usually thin saws set closely together are used. They must be kept well sharpened to avoid tearing out the narrow tongues of plywood remaining, and any vibration must be prevented if the correct depth of cut is to be maintained. The resulting piece of plywood, although requiring careful handling, can be bent to shape without further treatment. If a free standing bend is required, this may be made by gluing a cover veneer to the concave face during the bending operation and if the form is heated and a synthetic resin glue is used this can be done in a very short time.

One of the main disadvantages with this type of corner is that it is difficult to maintain a smooth outer surface, for flats tend to develop opposite the plywood tongues and ridges opposite the slots. Much can be done by spacing the slots carefully, but even then, if a highly polished convex face is required this effect can be troublesome.

(b) *The blocked corner*

Another method often used involves routing away most of the plywood where the bend is to be made. The routed area must be wide enough to ensure that when the bend is made its edges will be clear of the actual bent portion of the plywood and the depth of cut is such that no more than two plies remain on what is to become the convex face of the bend. A wooden block is carefully machined to

PLATE 26 *Some methods of making bent plywood corners*

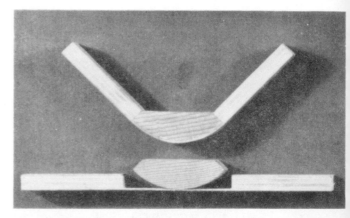

Inserted shaped solid block

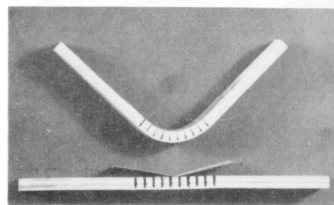

Saw kerf

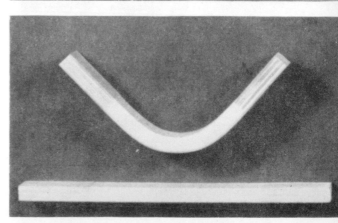

Without reinforcing veneer

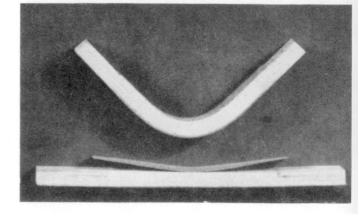

With reinforcing veneer

84

fit the routed space and is glued into position when the bend is made (*see Plate 26*). The plywood sheet again requires careful handling and some manipulation is necessary during the bending operation to ensure that the block does not jam across the edges of the routed portion and cause a breakage.

Accurate machining is necessary for success and the method tends to be wasteful of timber. The fact that it does not produce a continuous curve on the inner, concave face may also be a disadvantage in some cases.

(c) *The balsa corner*

A method similar to the above has been developed at the Forest Products Research Laboratory in which a low-density insert is used instead of the shaped block thus eliminating the need for a somewhat troublesome and time-consuming machining operation. The plywood to be bent is routed as before to leave only two plies or veneers, one of which may be the decorative face veneer. For best results, it is important to ensure that the face of the exposed veneer is absolutely clean and free from glue or fibres from the cutaway portion. A piece of low density timber such as balsa is now sawn and planed to fit and exactly fill the rectangular space cleared by routing, and with its grain running parallel to the axis of the bending former it is glued into position in the flat in a suitable press. If a synthetic resin glue is used and the press platens are heated, this will take no more than a few minutes. Any tendency for the assembly to dry out during this process can be easily offset by sponging the faces with water on removal from the press. The resulting composite material will be found to be very flexible and after a few hours' conditioning can be bent to the required shape (*see Plate 26*).

The actual bending operation can be carried out in suitable male and female forms or by any other convenient method but it is desirable that the surface of the form in contact with the concave face of the bend is heated as the insert then compresses more readily and less stress is induced in the plies comprising the convex face of the bend. If the face of the insert is moistened before bending and the assembly is left in contact with the hot form for a few minutes after the bend is completed, the assembly will be sufficiently set to shape for removal and incorporation in the finished article. If, however, a free-standing bend is required then a reinforcing veneer, covering the face of the insert and extending on to the plywood shoulders at each side, should be glued in position during the bending operation. For making bends of the sort

considered here with small radii of curvature, a very low density wood such as balsa will probably be required for the insert. With bends of larger radii, however, somewhat higher density material, for example a softwood such as Sitka spruce, could well prove suitable.

In the bending operation, the insert material is of course compressed on its concave face, and, tensile stresses are induced in the convex layers of the bend. When plywood faced with a decorative veneer is being bent along the grain practically the whole of this stress has to be withstood by this veneer and a certain amount of care needs to be exercised in its selection. However, the forces required to bend and compress the balsa wood insert are not high and tests have shown that most of the commonly used face veneers such as pencil-stripe walnut, oak and sapele in the usual 0·6 mm thickness possess adequate tensile strength. It would, however, be wise to carry out a few preliminary trials where highly decorative veneers such as burr walnut or bird's eye maple are concerned.

Although the method appears to find its main application in the bending of veneered plywood for such purposes as the construction of radio and television cabinets, wardrobes, sideboards and so on, it can be used equally effectively with metal-faced plywood, multi-ply and blockboard. Its main advantages are that the convex face of the bend is smooth and can take a high polish, the concave face is also curved, little machining is involved, and the process is not unduly wasteful of timber.

Appendices

I *Theoretical considerations*

Assessment of bending qualities from compressive and tensile stress-strain relationships

Since the process of bending consists essentially of compressing some and stretching other fibres of a piece of wood, theoretically, it should be possible to determine its bending properties and the bending forces involved from a knowledge of the simple stress-strain relationships of wood.

Such a method of determination involving the testing of small specimens in standard type testing machines would have obvious advantages over the direct method of testing comparatively large specimens on a specially designed bending machine. Moreover, it should also prove useful in the determination, not only of the limiting radii of curvature in bending both with and without a strap, but also of the bending moments and end-pressures set up in making a bend of any given radius and thickness. Consequently, a considerable number of experiments were carried out at the Forest Products Research Laboratory to ascertain whether, in fact, straightforward compression and tension tests could be made to yield reliable data relating to the bending properties of steamed wood, the problem being approached on the lines suggested by A. Prodehl in his treatise on the bending of steamed wood (see footnote page 95).

Fig. 36 has been drawn to represent a bending machine such as the one built for standard bending tests at the Laboratory, resembling somewhat the commercial machine for making walking sticks, which is shown in *Plate 10*. In this type of machine the form is caused to revolve and wrap the wood around itself, but the general principles and theoretical considerations involved in the bending process are the same as in the case of a machine in which the wood is wrapped around a stationary form. A fixed end-stop is clamped to the form and the other end-stop is fixed to the strap and is capable of moving only in the direction of the guide arm. The steel strap joining the two end-stops keeps the wood tightly pressed at the ends during the whole bending operation. The line 1–1 represents the end of the bent portion of the wood; the unbent portion lies between the lines o–o and 2–2. The latter is caused by the guide arm to move in a straight line up to the point of contact of the wood and form.

In the calculations given below the following assumptions were made

1 the originally plane cross-sections of the wood and strap remain plane during bending;
2 there is free movement between wood and metal strap;
3 the same stress distribution exists between each cross-section of the wood/strap system between the lines o–o and 2–2 of the diagram, *Fig. 36*;
4 the friction between wood and strap and wood and form may be neglected for the simplification of the calculations;
5 the thickness and stretch of the strong steel strap are small compared with those of the wood and can be neglected.

In the equation b is the breadth and l the length of the strap; B the breadth, S the thickness, and L the original length of the wood; p the intensity of stress, and e the strain in the wood and strap; r the radius of form and R the radius of the neutral axis of the bent wood; and β the bending angle, i.e. the angle subtended by the bent portion on the form.

End pressures

From the assumptions made, the uniform stress p in the still unbent portion of the wood between o–o and 2–2 gives a total pressure $-P$ (compressive) such that

$$-P = p.B.S. \qquad \ldots (1)$$

This force is transmitted to the strap, and since friction and the induced strains in the strap caused by bending of the metal may be neglected, the force P exists unchanged along the whole length of the strap.

Consider now a thin layer of wood of thickness dx on the curved portion between o–o and 1–1 at a distance $(r + x)$ from the centre of the form. Assuming this thin layer to have been originally of length y before bending, we get

$$\frac{r + x}{y(1 + e_x)} = \frac{R}{y}$$

$$\text{so } R(1 + e_x) = r + x \qquad \ldots (2)$$

and (differentiating)

$$Rde_x = dx \qquad \ldots (3)$$

The total pressure $-P$ in the bent portion of the wood is given as

$$-P = B\Sigma p_x dx \begin{array}{l} x=S \\ \\ x=o \end{array}$$

Now p is a function of e and is obtainable from the stress/strain curves of the wood in any given condition. Hence

$$p = f(e) \qquad \ldots (4)$$

89

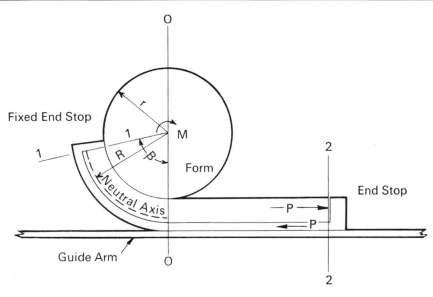

FIG 36 *Diagrammatic representation of a bending machine*

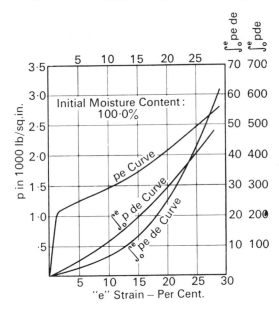

FIG 37 *Compressive stress/strain curves of steamed home-grown beech*

And substituting for p and dx we get

$$e = \left(\frac{r + S}{R} - 1\right)$$

$$-P = BR\Sigma f(e)\, de \qquad \qquad \ldots (5)$$

$$e = \left(\frac{r}{R} - 1\right)$$

Tension and compression tests

Tests for determining the stress/strain relationships of steamed wood both for compression and tension have been carried out at the Laboratory. Specimens $1 \times 1 \times 1\frac{3}{4}$ inch ($25 \times 25 \times 45$ mm) were cut and machined to provide material for determining the stress/strain relationships in compression, and these were compressed parallel to the grain and in the direction of the length.

The stress/strain relationships in tension were determined on specimens $1 \times \frac{1}{4}$ inch ($25 \times 6\cdot3$ mm) in cross-section and 10 inches (254 mm) in length.

All specimens were steamed in a small atmospheric steaming-oven situated close to the testing machine, and care was taken to ensure that the minimum heat loss occurred before the actual test was in progress.

The rate of straining in compression was $0\cdot15$ in/min ($3\cdot8$ mm/min) and in tension $0\cdot25$ in/min. ($6\cdot3$ mm/min).

The measurement of the tensile strain presented a certain amount of difficulty, and a special form of extensometer and multiplying device was developed for the purpose.

Typical stress-strain relationship curves ($p\ e$ curves) obtained for English beech, taken to the points where fractures occurred, are shown in *Figs. 37* and *38* and area curves are also shown on these graphs, and reference to these will be made later in the calculations.

Minimum radius

From such curves, an estimate of the minimum bending radius of curvature may be made in the following manner:

When an efficient strap with end pressure control is used, it may be taken that failure occurs only when limiting values of strain have been reached both in compression and tension.

If then $Y+$ represents this limiting strain value in tension and $Y-$ the limiting strain in compression, the length of the outer face of the bend will be given by $L\,(1 + Y+)$ and of the inner face by $L\,(1 + Y-)$, where L = initial length of specimen.

$$\therefore \frac{L(1 + Y_+)}{L(1 + Y_-)} = \frac{r + S}{r} \qquad \text{where } r = \text{radius and } S = \text{thickness}$$

$$\therefore \frac{S}{r} = \frac{Y_+ - Y_-}{1 + Y_-} \qquad \text{Note: } Y_- \text{ will have a negative value.}$$

Applying this formula to the limiting strain values given for beech on the curves we get

$$\frac{S}{r} = \frac{0\cdot0105 + 0\cdot29}{1 - 0\cdot29} = \frac{0\cdot3005}{0\cdot71}$$

Thus if $S = 1$ in., $r = \dfrac{0\cdot71}{0\cdot3005} = 2\cdot3$ in. (approximately)

The limiting radius allowing for one rejected bend in twenty, as determined in practice on this species from actual bending tests, was $1\cdot5$ in (see *Table 1*).

The estimation of the minimum radius without support may be arrived at by putting $P - O$ in equation (5) since end pressure here is zero. Thus

$$O = BR \int_{e = \frac{r}{R} - 1}^{e = Y_+} f(e)\,de$$

i.e. $\displaystyle\int_{e = o}^{e = Y_+} f(e)\,de = \int_{e = o}^{e = \frac{r}{R} - 1} f(e)\,de$

since $p = f(e)$ the value of $\displaystyle\int_{e = o}^{e = Y_+} f(e)\,de$ is given by the area under the stress/strain curve for the wood in tension which, in the example given, may be taken as being roughly $\frac{1}{2}\,(9500 \times 0\cdot0105) = 52$ units. It thus follows that tension failure is about to occur when

$$\int_{e = c}^{e = \frac{r}{R} - 1} f(e)\,de = 52,$$

and it remains to find the value of the compressive strain such that the area under the compressive stress/strain relationship curve is also given as 52 units. In the example given it will be found that this corresponds roughly with a compressive strain of 5 per cent ($-0\cdot05$).

Substituting in the equation $\dfrac{S}{r} = \dfrac{Y_+ - Y_-}{1 + Y_-}$ we now get

$$\frac{S}{r} = \frac{0.0105 + 0.05}{1 - 0.05} = \frac{0.06}{0.95}$$

from which $r = 16$ inches when $S = 1$ inch.

The minimum radius as determined in practice on this species (unsupported) was 13 inches (*see Table 1*).

Bending moments

The bending moment M of the wood/strap system referred to the centre of the form and, measured by the torque in the table, is given by the equation:

$$M = B \int_{x=0}^{x=S} p_x(r + x)dx + P(r + S)$$

Rewriting this we get:

$$M = rB \int_{x=0}^{x=S} p_x dx + B \int_{x=0}^{x=S} x p_x dx + P(r + S)$$

Now $rB \int_{x=0}^{x=S} p_x dx = -Pr$, and $x = R(1 + e_x) - r$ from (2)

$$\therefore M = -Pr + B \int_{x=0}^{x=S} R(1 + e_x)p_x dx - rB \int_{x=0}^{x=S} p_x dx + P(r+S)$$

$$= -Pr + RB \int_{x=0}^{x=S} p_x dx + BR \int_{x=\left(\frac{r}{R}-1\right)}^{x=\left(\frac{r+S}{R}-1\right)} Rf(e)e\,de + Pr + P(r + S)$$

$$= -RP + BR^2 \int_{e=\left(\frac{r}{R}-1\right)}^{e=\left(\frac{r+S}{R}-1\right)} f(e)e\,de + P(r + S)$$

$$= P(r + S - R) + BR^2 \int_{e=\left(\frac{r}{R}-1\right)}^{e=\left(\frac{r+S}{R}-1\right)} f(e)e\,de \qquad \ldots (6)$$

The equation for the bending moment given above consists of a couple, namely P multiplied by the distance between the neutral axis of the wood and the strap, plus a moment which varies as the square of the radius of the neutral axis of the wood.

The couple in the straight portion o—o to 2—2 is:

$$\frac{PS}{2}$$

This couple tends to cause the straight portion of the wood as it feeds on to the form to back-bend or 'snake', and it is to counteract this tendency that it is so necessary to provide bending straps with some form of back-plate. In the above equations, M and P, the bending moments and end-pressures, are given as functions of the unknown variable R, and it now remains to show the relation between R and β.

The strap length is assumed to remain unchanged; therefore, the distance between end-stops measured along the strap remains unaltered during bending.

Hence the distance d between o–o and 2–2 is given by:

$$d = L - \beta(r + S)$$

The bent length of the wood between o–o and 1–1 is given by βR

$$\therefore \beta R + \frac{d}{1 + e} = L$$

$$R = \frac{L(1 + e) - d}{\beta(1 + e)}$$

$$R = \frac{Le}{\beta(1 + e)} + \frac{r + S}{1 + e} \qquad \ldots (7)$$

End pressure values —P and bending moments M may now be found for any bending angle β from the stress/strain relationship curves, first by plotting the integral curve giving respectively the values of $\int p\,de$ and $\int p e\,de$ with the values of strain e as abscissae. Then by substituting arbitrary and numerous values of the radius of neutral axis R in equations (5) and (6), points on the curves giving the relationships between —P and R, also M and R, may be found and graphs plotted. Finally, by substituting the values of R and e in equation (7), the relationship between —P, M and β can be established.

Comparison between theoretical and actual bending values

In order to compare the calculated end pressures and bending moments with those obtained in actual practice, a bending machine was designed and built capable of measuring both end pressures and bending moments during the actual bending operation. This machine is illustrated in *Fig. 39* and consists of a revolving table A

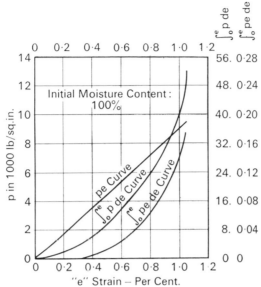

FIG 38 *Tensile stress/strain curves of steamed home-grown beech*

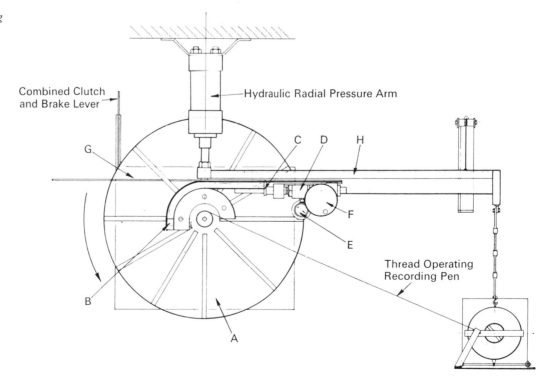

FIG 39 *Experimental wood bending machine at the Forest Products Research Laboratory*

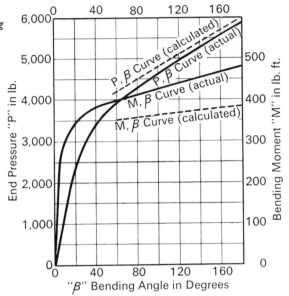

FIG 40 *The relationship between end pressures, bending moments and bending angle of home-grown beech*

to which is fitted the bending form complete with metal strap and fixed end-stop B. To the other end of the strap is fitted a movable end-stop C which is adjustable by means of a hand wheel and worm drive F. In this adjustable end-stop system is incorporated a glycerine-filled cylinder D and pressure gauge E in such a manner that the pressure exerted by the end of the wood on the stop may be measured at any instant during bending.

This complete end-stop system, including a back-plate G, is free to slide along a guide arm H over a series of rollers. This guide arm is supported at either end on rollers, one set resting on the table and the other on a trestle. A hydraulic radial pressure arm and roller is arranged so as to press on the wood at the point of bending, and in this way to keep the bend pressed tightly to the face of the form.

The guide arm is pivoted at one end to this radial pressure arm and, at the other, is fastened to a spring-loaded balance in such a manner that the back thrust or the resistance to bending of the piece can be measured. This balance pull is registered automatically on a chart and plotted against the angle through which the wood has been bent at any instant, so that by multiplying the reading by the length of the guide arm, the bending moment may be determined.

Some typical curves showing the relationship between end pressures, bending moments and bending angle for English beech specimens 3 ft (0·9m) long, 3 inches (75 mm) wide and 1½ inches (38 mm) thick, bent to a radius of curvature of 8 inches (200 mm), are given in *Fig. 40*. Calculated or theoretical curves determined from results of straightforward compression and tension tests on matched material are also shown in the figure in dotted form, from which some idea of the discrepancies between the two as obtained on the beech samples tested may be formed.

Comments

The method of determining the bending properties of steamed wood by standard type compression and tension tests, though economical in timber, could not be considered to yield results reliable or even reasonably accurate in practice.

The reasons for the discrepancies became apparent when it was observed in the actual bending operation that (a) initially plane sections did not remain plane, (b) friction between the wood and strap might become appreciable in amount, and (c) the radial pressures exerted by the

strap often resulted in appreciable thinning of the section.

Still more serious difficulties arose in testing some of the exotic timbers of inferior bending qualities, when it was found virtually impossible to decide exactly at what stage during the compression of the test pieces failure occurred. Nevertheless, such tests often do provide some indication of the bending properties of timber and may yield data from which a better understanding of the principles of bending may be obtained.

It is, for example, interesting to note that the radius of the neutral axis in the wood varies with angle of bend and tends to increase with increase in this angle. In making heavy bends, the neutral axis may well reach the convex face, in which case all the wood is in compression. It is in order to reduce somewhat the extent of this compression, and hence the liability to compression failure, that it often becomes advisable to reduce the end pressure by slackening off the adjustable end-stop and allowing as much stretch to take place as is possible without fracture. Again, it is possible to show theoretically how local stretching at the commencement of certain heavy bends, using straps with fixed end-stops, may be enough to cause fracture, in which case it will prove beneficial to adjust the end-stop initially so that pressure is applied to the wood before any of it is actually bent.

Untersuchungen über das biegen Gedämpften Holzes. (Rotaprint von der Sächsischen Technischen Hochschule, Dresden.)

2 Tables

Table 1 *Limiting Radii of Curvature of Various Species in Steam Bending (Air-dried steamed material 1 inch (25·4 mm) thick)*

Species		Radius in inches		Radius in millimetres	
Standard name	Botanical name	Supported by a strap	Unsupported	Supported by a strap	Unsupported
Abura	*Mitragyna ciliata*	31·0	35·0	790	890
Acacia, False	see *Robinia*				
'African Walnut'	*Lovoa trichilioides*	18·0	32·0	460	810
Afrormosia	*Pericopsis elata*	14·0	29·0	360	740
*Afzelia	*Afzelia bipindensis*	18·0	34·0	460	860
Afzelia (mbembakofi)	*Afzelia quanzensis*	9·0	14·0	230	360
Agba	*Gossweilerodendron balsamiferum*	20·0	16·0	510	410
Agboin	see Dahoma				
Albizia	*Albizia ferruginea*	20·0	40·0	510	1020
Alder	*Alnus glutinosa*	14·0	18·0	360	460
*Alstonia	*Alstonia congensis*	31·0	—	790	—
*Anopyxis	*Anopyxis ealaensis*	40·0	60·0	1020	1520
Ash, American	*Fraxinus* sp.	4·5	13·0	110	330
Ash, European (home-grown)	*Fraximus excelsior*	2·5	12·0	64	300
Ash, European (French)	*Fraxinus* sp.	2·0	13·5	51	340
Avodire	*Turraeanthus africanus*	36·0	38·0	910	970
Ayan	*Distemonanthus benthamianus*	20·0	32·0	510	810
*Banak	*Virola koschnyi*	30·0	48·0	760	1220
Beech, European (Danish)	*Fagus sylvatica*	1·7	14·5	43	370
Beech, European (Rumanian)	*Fagus sylvatica*	1·6	16·0	41	410
Beech, European (home-grown)	*Fagus sylvatica*	1·5	13·0	38	330
*'Beech, Southland'	see 'silver beech'				
Berlinia	*Berlinia* sp.	17·5	19·5	440	500
Binuang	*Octomeles sumatrana*	37·0	36·0	940	910
*Birch, Canadian Yellow	*Betula alleghaniensis*	3·0	17·0	76	430
*Blackbutt	*Eucalyptus pilularis*	24·0	48·0	610	1220
Bosse	see *Guarea*				
*Cabbage-bark, Black	*Lonchocarpus castilloi*	30·0	—	760	—
*'Camphorwood, East African'	see 'East African camphorwood'				
Canarium, African	*Canarium schweinfurthii*	34·0	35·0	860	890
'Cedar, Port Orford' (imported)	see 'Port Orford cedar'				
*Cedar, Western Red (home-grown)	see 'Western Red Cedar'				
Celtis, African	*Celtis* sp.	10·5	34·0	270	860
Cherry, European (home-grown)	*Prunus avium*	2·0	17·0	51	430
Chestnut, Horse	see Horse-chestnut				
Chestnut, Sweet	*Castanea sativa*	6·0	15·0	150	380
'Chilean laurel'	*Laurelia aromatica*	17·0	19·5	430	500
*Coigue	*Nothofagus dombeyi*	10·0	16·5	250	420
Courbaril	*Hymenaea courbaril*	12·5	31·0	320	790
*Crabwood	*Carapa guianensis*	30·0	48·0	760	1220

*Denotes that limiting radius of curvature of species has been derived from results of very small-scale tests only

Table 1 *Cont*

Species		Radius in inches		Radius in millimetres	
Standard name	Botanical name	Supported by a strap	Unsupported	Supported by a strap	Unsupported
*Cramantee	*Guarea excelsa*	18·0	32·0	460	810
*Cypress, Leyland (home-grown)	*Cupressocyparis (Cupressus) leylandii*	28·0	32·0	710	810
Dahoma	*Piptadeniastrum africanum*	15·0	29·0	380	740
Dahoma (mpewere)	*Piptadeniastrum africanum*	11·0	27·0	280	690
Daniellia	see Ogea				
Danta	*Nesogordonia papaverifera*	14·0	30·0	360	760
'Douglas Fir' (home-grown)	*Pseudotsuga menziesii*	18·0	33·0	460	840
*'East African Camphorwood'	*Ocotea usambarensis*	14·0	27·0	360	690
Ebony, African	*Diospyros crassiflora*	10·0	15·0	250	380
Ekhimi	see Dahoma				
Elm, Dutch (home-grown)	*Ulmus hollandica*	<0·5	9·5	13	240
Elm, English	*Ulmus procera*	1·5	13·5	38	340
Elm, Rock	*Ulmus thomasii*	1·5	14·0	38	360
Elm, White	*Ulmus americana*	1·7	13·5	43	340
Elm, Wych	*Ulmus glabra*	1·7	12·5	43	320
*Eng	*Dipterocarpus tuberculatus*	11·0	32·0	280	810
Erimado	*Ricinodendron heudelotii*	48·0	34·0	1220	860
Esia	*Combretodendron macrocarpum*	36·0	27·0	910	690
'Fir, Douglas' (home-grown)	see 'Douglas Fir'				
*Gedu nohor	*Entandrophragma angolense*	24·0	40·0	610	1020
Grand Fir (home-grown)	*Abies grandis*	36·0	36·0	910	910
Greenheart	*Ocotea rodiaei*	18·0	36·0	460	910
*Guarea	*Guarea thompsonii*	14·0	36·0	360	910
Guarea, Scented	*Guarea cedrata*	7·5	20·0	190	510
*Gurjun (Ceylon and India)	*Dipterocarpus* spp.	30·0	—	760	—
Hemlock, Western (home-grown)	*Tsuga heterophylla*	19·0	36·0	480	910
Hickory	*Carya* sp.	1·8	15·0	46	380
Hornbeam (home-grown)	*Carpinus betulus*	4·0	16·5	100	420
Horse-chestnut, European	*Aesculus hippocastanum*	6·0	18·0	150	460
Idigbo	*Terminalia ivorensis*	32·0	44·0	810	1120
Iroko	*Chlorophora excelsa*	15·0	18·0	380	460
*Jarrah	*Eucalyptus marginata*	17·5	39·0	440	990
Kapur, Sabah	*Dryobalanops lanceolata*	17·0	30·0	430	760
*Karri (South African)	*Eucalyptus diversicolor*	8·0	12·5	200	320
Keruing, Sabah	*Dipterocarpus acutangulus*	16·0	37·0	410	940
	Dipterocarpus caudiferus	17·0	29·0	430	740
Kokrodua	see Afrormosia				
Krabak	see Mersawa				
Kurokai	*Protium decandrum*	16·5	29·0	420	740
Larch, European (home-grown)	*Larix decidua*	13·0	18·0	330	460

*Denotes that limiting radius of curvature of species has been derived from results of very small-scale tests only

Table 1 *Cont*

Species		Radius in inches		Radius in millimetres	
Standard name	Botanical name	Supported by a strap	Unsupported	Supported by a strap	Unsupported
Larch, Japanese (home-grown)	*Larix leptolepis*	16·5	31·0	420	790
'Laurel, Chilean'	see 'Chilean Laurel'				
Lime, European (home-grown)	*Tilia vulgaris*	14·0	16·0	360	410
*Louro preto	*Ocotea* or *Nectandra* sp.	20·0	—	510	—
Mahogany, African (Ghana)	*Khaya anthotheca*	36·0	32·0	910	810
Mahogany, African (Uganda)	*Khaya anthotheca*	20·0	24·0	510	610
Mahogany, African	*Khaya grandifoliola*	33·0	36·0	840	910
Mahogany, African	*Khaya ivorensis*	38·0	35·0	970	890
*Mahogany, American (Indian grown)	*Swietenia macrophylla*	12·0	28·0	300	710
Makore	*Tieghemella heckelii*	12·0	18·0	300	460
Mansonia	*Mansonia altissima*	10·0	15·5	250	390
Mbembakofi	see *Afzelia*				
*Mchenga	*Julbernardia globiflora*	15·0	32·0	380	810
Mersawa	*Anisoptera* spp.	30·0	28·0	760	710
Mjombo	*Brachystegia? boehmii*	25·0	35·0	640	890
*Mkwaju	*Tamarindus indica*	12·5	33·0	320	840
Mora	*Mora excelsa*	13·0	32·0	330	810
Morabukea	*Mora gonggrijpii*	11·5	32·0	290	810
Mpwere	see Dahoma				
Mtondo	*Brachystegia? spiciformis*	32·0	40·0	810	1020
Mubura	*Parinari excelsa*	13·0	32·0	330	810
Muchenche	*Newtonia buchanani*	30·0	33·0	760	840
Muhimbi	*Cynometra alexandri*	16·5	37·0	420	940
Muhuhu	*Brachylaena hutchinsii*	18·0	36·0	460	910
Mulberry, East African	*Morus lactea*	7·0	18·0	180	460
Muninga	*Pterocarpus angolensis*	16·5	18·0	420	460
Munyama	see Mahogany, African (*Khaya anthotheca*)				
Musheragi	see Olive, East African				
*Musizi	*Maesopsis eminii*	40·0	60·0	1020	1520
Mutenye	*Guibourtia arnoldiana*	15·0	27·0	380	690
Mvule	see Iroko				
Nargusta	*Terminalia amazonia*	30·0	—	760	—
Niangon	*Tarrietia utilis*	18·0	30·0	460	760
Oak, American White	*Quercus* spp.	0·5	13·0	13	330
Oak, European (home-grown)	*Quercus robur*	2·0	13·0	51	330
Oak, Japanese	*Quercus* spp.	1·5	12·5	38	320
Oak, Red (home-grown)	*Quercus rubra*	1·0	11·5	25	290
Oak, Turkey (home-grown)	*Quercus cerris*	3·5	11·0	89	280
Obeche	*Triplochiton scleroxylon*	18·0	17·0	460	430

*Denotes that limiting radius of curvature of species has been derived from results of very small-scale tests only

Table 1 *Cont*

Species		Radius in inches		Radius in millimetres	
Standard name	Botanical name	Supported by a strap	Unsupported	Supported by a strap	Unsupported
*Odoko	*Scottellia coriacea*	30·0	60·0	760	1520
Ogea	*Daniellia ogea*	50·0	28·0	1270	710
Okwen	*Brachystegia nigerica*	13·0	34·0	330	860
Olive, East African	*Olea hochstetteri*	11·5	30·0	290	760
Opepe	*Nauclea diderrichii*	28·0	37·0	710	940
'Port Orford' cedar (imported)	*Chamaecyparis lawsoniana*	34·0	18·0	860	460
Pillarwood	*Cassipourea malosana*	8·0	21·0	200	530
*Pine, Caribbean Pitch	*Pinus caribaea*	14·0	28·0	360	710
Pine, Corsican (home-grown)	*Pinus nigra* var. *calabrica*	34·0	29·0	860	740
Plane, European (home-grown)	*Platanus hybrida*	2·0	17·0	51	430
*Podo	*Podocarpus* spp.	18·0	20·0	460	510
Poplar (French)	*Populus* sp.	32·0	26·0	810	660
Pterygota, African	*Pterygota bequaertii*	36·0	33·0	910	840
Purpleheart	*Peltogyne* spp.	18·0	30·0	460	760
'Queensland walnut'	*Endiandra palmerstonii*	20·0	44·0	510	1120
Ramin	*Gonystylus bancanus*	36·0	37·0	910	940
Rauli	*Nothofagus procera*	16·5	16·5	420	420
'Rhodesian teak'	*Baikiaea plurijuga*	13·0	25·0	330	640
Robinia (home-grown)	*Robinia pseudoacacia*	1·5	11·0	38	280
Santa Maria (British Honduras)	*Calophyllum brasiliense* var. *rekoi*	20·0	56·0	510	1420
Sapele	*Entandrophragma cylindricum*	30·0	37·0	760	940
Sepetir	*Pseudosindora palustris*	18·0	37·0	460	940
Seraya, Light Red	*Shorea leptoclados*	28·0	33·0	710	840
	Shorea parvifolia	35·0	37·0	890	940
	Shorea smithiana	36·0	36·0	910	910
	Shorea waltonii	35·0	28·0	890	710
Seraya, Dark Red	*Shorea pauciflora*	30·0	36·0	760	910
Seraya, White	*Parashorea malaanonan*	33·0	35·0	840	890
*Seraya, Yellow	*Shorea* spp.	18·0	31·0	460	790
Serrette	*Byrsonima coriacea* var. *spicata*	17·0	35·0	430	890
*'Silver Beech'	*Nothofagus menziesii*	10·0	20·0	250	510
Spruce European (home-grown)	*Picea abies*	37·0	29·0	940	740
Spruce, Sitka (home-grown)	*Picea sitchensis*	36·0	32·0	910	810
Sterculia, Brown	*Sterculia rhinopetala*	12·0	14·0	300	360
Sterculia, Yellow	*Sterculia oblonga*	17·0	18·5	430	470
Sycamore (home-grown)	*Acer pseudoplatanus*	1·5	14·5	38	370
'Tasmanian myrtle'	*Nothofagus cunninghamii*	7·0	17·0	180	430
*'Tasmanian oak'	*Eucalyptus obliqua*	16·0	24·0	410	610
	Eucalyptus regnans	30·0	30·0	760	760
Teak (Burma)	*Tectona grandis*	18·0	35·0	460	890

*Denotes that limiting radius of curvature of species has been derived from results of very small-scale tests only

Table 1 *Cont*

Species		Radius in inches		Radius in millimetres	
Standard name	Botanical name	Supported by a strap	Unsupported	Supported by a strap	Unsupported
Teak (W. Nigeria)	*Tectona grandis*	10·0	26·0	250	660
Teak (N. Nigeria)	*Tectona grandis*	18·0	35·0	460	890
'Teak, Rhodesian'	see 'Rhodesian teak'				
Utile (Uganda-mfumbi)	*Entandrophragma utile*	36·0	40·0	910	1020
*Waika chewstick	*Symphonia globulifera*	28·0	—	710	—
Wallaba	*Eperua falcata*	16·0	33·0	410	840
'Walnut, African'	see 'African Walnut'				
Walnut, European (home-grown)	*Juglans regia*	1·0	11·0	25	280
'Walnut, Queensland'	see 'Queensland Walnut				
Wamara	*Swartzia leiocalycina*	15·5	29·0	390	740
'Western Red Cedar' (home-grown)	*Thuja plicata*	35·0	37·0	890	940
White Olivier	see Nargusta				
*Yellowwood, British Honduras	*Podocarpus guatemalensis*	35·0	36·0	890	910
*Yemeri	*Vochysia hondurensis*	30·0	40·0	760	1020
Yew	*Taxus baccata*	8·5	16·5	220	420

*Denotes that limiting radius of curvature of species has been derived from results of very small-scale tests only

Table 2 *Limiting Radii of Curvature of Thin Laminations (Material ⅛ inch (3·2 mm) thick at 12 per cent Moisture content)*

Species		Radius		Approx. ratio:radius/ lamination thickness
Standard Name	Botanical Name	(in)	(mm)	
Abura	*Mitragyna ciliata*	6·0	152	48
Acacia, False	See *Robinia*	—		
'African Walnut'	*Lovoa trichilioides*	6·0	152	48
Afrormosia	*Pericopsis elata*	6·5	165	52
Afzelia	*Afzelia bipindensis*	9·5	241	76
Afzelia (mbembakofi)	*Afzelia quanzensis*	7·1	180	57
Agba	*Gossweilerodendron balsamiferum*	4·4	112	35
Agboin	See Dahoma	—		
Albizia	*Albizia ferruginea*	7·0	178	56
Alder	*Alnus glutinosa*	7·4	188	59
Ash, European (home-grown)	*Fraxinus excelsior*	4·8	122	38
Ash, European (French)	*Fraxinus* sp.	4·8	122	38
Avodire	*Turraeanthus africanus*	7·2	183	58
Ayan	*Distemonanthus benthamianus*	7·3	185	58
Baromalli	*Catostemma commune*	6·3	160	50
Beech, European (Danish)	*Fagus sylvatica*	5·3	135	42
Beech, European (Rumanian)	*Fagus sylvatica*	4·5	114	36
Beech, European (home-grown)	*Fagus sylvatica*	4·4	112	35
Berlinia	*Berlinia* sp.	5·4	137	43
Binuang	*Octomeles sumatrana*	7·3	185	58
'Camphorwood, Borneo'	See Kapur	—		
'Camphorwood, East African'	*Ocotea usambarensis*	6·9	175	55
Canarium	*Canarium schweinfurthii*	7·4	188	59
'Cedar, Port Orford' (imported)	*Chamaecyparis lawsoniana*	7·4	188	59
Cedar, Western Red (home-grown)	see Western Red Cedar	—	—	—
Celtis, African	*Celtis* sp.	6·6	168	53
Cherry, European (home-grown)	*Prunus avium*	5·9	150	47
Chestnut, Horse	See Horse-chestnut	—		
Chestnut, Sweet	*Castanea sativa*	7·5	191	60
Coigue	*Nothofagus dombeyi*	6·4	163	51
Courbaril	*Hymenaea courbaril*	8·4	214	67
Cypress, European (home-grown)	*Cupressocyparis (Cupressus) leylandii*	4·0	102	32
Dahoma (West Africa) (Agboin)	*Piptadeniastrum africanum*	8·5	216	68
Dahoma (East Africa) (mpewere)	*Piptadeniastrum africanum*	8·0	203	64
Daniellia	See Ogea	—		
Danta	*Nesogordonia papaverifera*	5·3	135	42
'Douglas, Fir' (home-grown)	*Pseudotsuga menziesii*	7·8	198	62
'Douglas Fir (imported)	*Pseudotsuga menziesii*	5·9	150	47
Ebony, African	*Diospyros crassiflora*	5·1	130	41
Ekhimi	See Dahoma	—		

Table 2 *Cont*

Species		Radius		Approx. ratio:radius/ lamination thickness
Standard Name	Botanical Name	(in)	(mm)	
Elm, Dutch (home-grown)	*Ulmus hollandica*	3·9	99	31
Elm, English	*Ulmus procera*	5·8	147	46
Elm, Rock	*Ulmus thomasii*	3·9	99	31
Elm, White	*Ulmus americana*	4·3	109	34
Elm, Wych	*Ulmus glabra*	4·6	117	37
Erimado	*Ricinodendron heudelotii*	7·5	191	60
Esia	*Combretodendron macrocarpum*	6·4	163	51
'Fir, Douglas' (home-grown)	See 'Douglas Fir'	—		
Freijo	*Corida goeldiana*	7·3	185	58
Grand Fir	*Abies grandis*	10·0	254	80
Greenheart	*Ocotea rodiaei*	7·3	185	58
Guarea, Scented (bosse)	*Guarea cearata*	7·9	201	63
Hemlock, Western (home-grown)	*Tsuga heterophylla*	8·8	223	70
Hickory	*Carya* sp.	5·8	147	46
Hornbeam (home-grown)	*Carpinus betulus*	5·5	140	44
Horse-chestnut, European	*Aesculus hippocastanum*	5·0	127	40
Idigbo	*Terminalia ivorensis*	7·5	191	60
Iroko	*Chlorophora excelsa*	8·3	211	66
Jarrah	*Eucalyptus marginata*	6·8	173	54
Kapur, Sabah	*Dryobalanops lanceolata*	6·8	173	54
Keruing, Sabah	*Dipterocarpus acutangulus*	5·8	147	46
	Dipterocarpus caudiferus	6·5	165	52
Kokrodua	See Afrormosia	—		
Krabak	See Mersawa	—		
Kurokai	*Protium decandrum*	6·7	170	54
Larch, European (home-grown)	*Larix decidua*	6·0	152	48
Larch, Japanese (home-grown)	*Larix leptolepis*	7·9	201	63
'Laurel, Chilean'	*Laurelia aromatica*	6·8	173	54
Lime, European (home-grown)	*Tilia vulgaris*	7·0	178	56
Maho	*Sterculia pruriens*	6·5	165	52
Mahogany, African (Ghana)	*Khaya anthotheca*	6·8	173	54
Mahogany, African (Uganda)	*Khaya anthotheca*	5·8	147	46
Mahogany, African	*Khaya grandifoliola*	8·5	216	68
Mahogany, African	*Khaya ivorensis*	9·3	236	74
Mahogany, Sapele	See Sapele	—		
Makore	*Tieghemella heckelii*	6·2	157	50
Mansonia	*Mansonia altissima*	4·3	109	34
Maple, Field	*Acer campestre*	6·4	163	51
Mbembakofi	See Afzelia	—		
Mchenga	*Julbernardia globiflora*	6·8	173	54

Tables

Table 2 *Cont*

Species		Radius		Approx. ratio:radius/ lamination thickness
Standard Name	Botanical Name	(in)	(mm)	
Mersawa	*Anisoptera* spp.	7·0	178	56
Mjombo	*Brachystegia? boehmii*	6·8	173	54
Mkwaju	*Tamarindus indica*	6·9	175	55
Mora	*Mora excelsa*	6·1	155	49
Morabukea	*Mora gonggrijpii*	9·5	241	76
Mpwere	See Dahoma (East Africa)	—		
Mtondo	*Brachystegia? spiciformis*	7·3	185	58
Mubura	*Parinari excelsa*	6·5	165	52
Muchenche	*Newtonia buchanani*	8·8	224	70
Muhimbi	*Cynometra alexandri*	7·3	185	58
Muhuhu	*Brachylaena hutchinsii*	10·3	262	82
Mulberry, East African	*Morus lactea*	6·8	173	54
Muninga	*Pterocarpus angolensis*	6·8	173	54
Munyama	See Mahogany, African (*Khaya anthotheca*)	—		
Musheragi	See Olive, East African	—		
Mutenye	*Guibourtia arnoldiana*	7·0	178	56
Mvule	See Iroko	—		
Niangon	*Tarrietia utilis*	7·4	188	59
Oak, American White	*Quercus* spp.	5·4	137	43
Oak, European (home grown)	*Quercus robur*	5·8	147	46
Oak, Japanese	*Quercus* spp.	5·4	137	43
Oak Red (home-grown)	*Quercus rubra*	4·4	112	35
Oak, Turkey (home-grown)	*Quercus cerris*	4·5	114	36
Obeche	*Triplochiton scleroxylon*	6·0	152	48
Ogea	*Daniellia ogea*	8·4	213	67
Okwen	*Brachystegia nigerica*	7·4	188	59
Olive, East African	*Olea hochstetteri*	7·4	188	59
Opepe	*Nauclea diderrichii*	10·9	277	87
Pillarwood	*Cassipourea malosana*	4·6	117	37
Pine, Corsican (home-grown)	*Pinus nigra* var *calabrica*	5·9	150	47
Plane, European	*Platanus acerifolia*	5·3	135	42
Poplar (French)	*Populus* sp.	6·3	160	50
Pterygota	*Pterygota bequaertii*	6·1	155	49
Purpleheart	*Peltogyne* spp.	8·0	203	64
'Queensland walnut'	*Endiandra palmerstonii*	7·4	188	59
Ramin	*Gonystylus* sp.	9·0	229	72
Rauli	*Nothofagus procera*	7·5	191	60
Redwood, Baltic	*Pinus sylvestris*	6·9	175	55
'Rhodesian teak'	*Baikiaea plurijuga*	6·5	165	52
Roble (home-grown)	*Nothofagus obliqua*	5·4	137	43

Table 2 *Cont*

Species		Radius		Approx. ratio:radius/ lamination thickness
Standard Name	Botanical Name	(in)	(mm)	
Saligna Gum	*Eucalyptus saligna*	9·3	236	74
Sapele	*Entandrophragma cylindricum*	6·3	160	50
Sepetir	*Pseudosindora palustris*	7·1	180	57
Seraya, Light Red	*Shorea leptoclados*	8·0	203	64
	Shorea parvifolia	7·5	191	60
	Shorea smithiana	7·3	185	58
	Shorea waltonii	5·9	150	47
Seraya, Dark Red	*Shorea pauciflora*	6·5	165	52
Seraya, White	*Parashorea malaanonan*	7·8	198	62
Seraya, Yellow	*Shorea* spp.	5·9	150	47
Serrette	*Byrsonima coriacea* var. *spicata*	7·4	188	59
Spruce, European (home-grown)	*Picea abies*	7·8	198	62
Spruce, Sitka (home-grown)	*Picea sitchensis*	5·4	137	43
Sterculia, Brown	*Sterculia rhinopetala*	4·5	114	36
Sterculia, Yellow	*Sterculia oblonga*	6·4	163	51
Sycamore (home-grown)	*Acer pseudoplatanus*	4·0	102	32
'Tasmanian myrtle'	*Nothofagus cunninghamii*	6·1	155	49
Teak (Burma)	*Tectona grandis*	6·3	160	50
Teak (W. Nigeria)	*Tectona grandis*	5·8	147	46
Teak (N. Nigeria)	*Tectona grandis*	6·5	165	52
'Teak Rhodesian'	See 'Rhodesian teak'	—		
Utile (Uganda mfumbi)	*Entandrophragma utile*	8·3	211	66
Wallaba	*Eperua falcata*	11·0	279	88
'Walnut, African'	See 'African Walnut'	—		
Walnut, European (home-grown)	*Juglans regia*	3·6	91	29
'Walnut, Queensland'	See 'Queensland Walnut'	—		
Wamara	*Swartzia leiocalycina*	7·0	178	56
Western Red Cedar	*Thuja plicata*	8·0	203	64
Yew	*Taxus baccata*	6·8	173	54

Table 3 *The effect of the 'Loose' Face in Sliced Laminations* 0·10 *in* (2·5 *mm*) *thick on the Limiting Radius of Curvature*

Species	Average moisture content	Position of 'loose' face in bend	Radius at which losses due to breakages did not exceed 5% of the pieces bent		Approximate ratio: radius/ thickness of lamination
	(%)		(in)	(mm)	
Sitka Spruce (*Picea sitchensis*)	14·0	Tension side	9·3	233	93
		Compression side	6·5	165	65
Western Hemlock (*Tsuga heterophylla*)	13·3	Tension side	7·4	188	74
		Compression side	5·3	135	53
Douglas Fir (*Pseudotsuga menziesii*)	13·2	Tension side	9·0	229	90
		Compression side	8·5	216	85

Table 4 *The Effect of Immersion in Boiling Water on the Limiting Radius of Curvature of Laminations* ⅛ *in* (3·2 *mm*) *thick*

Species	Treatment	Radius at which losses due to breakages did not exceed 5% of the pieces bent		Approximate ratio: radius/ thickness of lamination
		(in)	(mm)	
Elm, Dutch (home-grown)	None.	3·9	99	31
(*Ulmus hollandica* var. *major*)	Immersed in boiling water for 30 minutes.	1·0	25	8
Beech (home-grown) (*Fagus sylvatica*)	None.	4·4	112	35
	Immersed in boiling water for 30 minutes	1·6	41	13
Oak (home-grown) (*Quercus robur*)	None.	5·8	147	46
	Immersed in boiling water for 30 minutes	1·5	38	12
Spruce, Sitka (*Picea sitchensis*)	None.	6·0	152	48
	Immersed in boiling water for 30 minutes	3·4	86	27

Table 5 *The Effect of Lamination Thickness on the Radius of Curvature of Baltic Redwood*

Thickness of Lamination	Moisture Content	Direction of Growth Rings*	Radius (inches) and corresponding percentage breakages				Ratio: radius/ thickness (At which 5% breakages occur)
(in)	(%)		5%	10%	15%	20%	
⅛	11·8	S	5·0	4·6	4·0	3·8	40·0
		Q	4·6	4·3	4·1	3·9	36·8
¼	11·9	Q	12·1	10·7	9·8	9·3	48·4
½	11·6	Q	28·1	25·2	24·2	23·7	56·2
¾	12·1	Q	41·0	36·3	35·0	33·0	54·7

*S – Growth rings parallel to the axis of the bend (slash cut)

Q – Growth rings perpendicular to the axis of the bend (quarter cut)

Table 6 *Approximate Ratio of Radius of Curvature to Lamination Thickness (R/S) for Structural Laminations Bent Dry (12% m.c. approx)*

Species	Ratio: Radius (R)/ Thickness (S)
'Douglas Fir'	125
Larch, European	110
Scots pine	85
Sitka spruce	115
Western hemlock	120
Agba	80
Ash	85
Beech	80
Danta	95
Elm Rock,	70
Greenheart	130
Gurjun	135
Idigbo	135
Iroko	150
Mahogany, African	110
Makore	110
Oak, home-grown	100
Opepe	195
Ramin	160
Teak	110
Utile	150

Table 7 *Relationship between Relative Humidity and Temperature of the Air and Equilibrium Moisture Content of Wood*

Equilibrium Moisture Content	Dry Bulb Temperature (°c)	Wet Bulb Temperature (°c)	Relative Humidity (%)
12%	15	10·5	54
	25	19·5	58
	35	29·0	62
	65	58·5	73
15%	15	12·0	68
	25	21·5	71
	35	31·0	75
	65	61·0	83
18%	15	13·0	79
	25	22·5	82
	35	32·5	84
	65	63·5	93

Table 8 *The effect of Thickness on the Ratio, Radius of Curvature: Thickness, for Plywood Bent Cold and Along the Grain*

African Mahogany			Finnish Birch			
Thickness	Radius*	Radius/ Thickness	Thickness	Radius*		Radius/ Thickness
	(in.)		(mm)	(in.)	(mm)	
$\frac{3}{64}$ in.	1·0	21·3	—	—	—	—
$\frac{3}{32}$ in.	2·6	27·7	4 mm	5·7	145	36·5
$\frac{3}{16}$ in.	6·5	34·7	6 mm	9·8	249	41·5
$\frac{3}{8}$ in.	16·1	42·9	9 mm	18·1	460	51·0

*The radius at which breakages did not exceed 5%

Table 9 *Limiting Radii of Curvature for Species of Plywood (Material $\frac{3}{16}$ in (4·8 mm) thickness)*

Species		Grain Direc- tion*	Bent Cold			Bent 'Softened' by Boiling		
Standard Name	Botanical Name		Moisture Content (%)	Radius† (in)	(mm)	Moisture Content (%)	Radius† (in)	(mm)
Afara	*Terminalia superba*	L	11·2	10·2	259	59·1	3·2	81
		T	11·7	4·9	124	60·0	1·0	25
Agba	*Gossweilerodendron*	L	10·4	9·2	234	45·9	1·9	48
	balsamiferum	T	9·7	7·5	191	67·3	0·8	20
Alder	*Alnus glutinosa*	L	8·4	11·0	279	—	—	—
		T	—	—	—	—	—	—
Beech (home-grown)	*Fagus sylvatica*	L	10·5	5·0	127	—	—	—
		T	—	—	—	—	—	—
Birch, Canadian	*Betula alleghaniensis*	L	10·9	4·4	112	65·5	0·9	23
		T	—	—	—	—	—	—
Birch‡, Finnish	*Betula* spp.	L	10·8	5·7	145	—	—	—
		T	11·2	3·5	89	—	—	—
'Fir, Douglas'	*Pseudotsuga menziesii*	L	10·2	15·3	389	—	—	—
		T	—	—	—	—	—	—
Gaboon	*Aucoumea klaineana*	L	9·3	8·5	216	64·3	3·1	79
		T	9·3	4·4	112	70·2	0·6	15
Mahogany, African	*Khaya ivorensis*	L	9·8	6·5	165	37·6	1·9	48
		T	10·0	3·8	97	40·3	0·7	18
Makore	*Tieghemella heckelii*	L	9·3	9·5	241	30·5	2·2	56
		T	9·1	3·4	86	31·2	0·7	18
'Pine, Chile'	*Araucaria araucana*	L	12·6	8·4	213	80·9	3·7	94
		T	12·4	2·5	64	97·3	0·6	15

Table 9 *Cont*

Species		Grain Direc-tion*	Bent Cold			Bent 'Softened' by Boiling		
Standard Name	Botanical Name		Moisture Content (%)	Radius† (in)	(mm)	Moisture Content (%)	Radius† (in)	(mm)
Pine, Scots	*Pinus sylvestris*	L	9·4	16·0	406	60·5	4·5	114
		T	9·4	4·9	124	57·6	1·0	25
Poplar	*Populus nigra*	L	10·0	10·2	259	108·8	3·0	76
		T	9·4	3·4	86	102·9	0·6	15
Pterygota	*Pterygota bequaertii*	L	9·9	7·5	191	38·8	3·0	76
		T	9·7	3·0	76	39·2	0·7	18
Sapele	*Entandrophragma cylindricum*	L	11·2	8·7	221	48·8	3·3	84
		T	10·7	3·4	86	46·9	0·8	20
Seraya, Red	*Shorea* spp.	L	11·4	8·0	203	56·4	3·7	94
		T	11·1	4·0	102	78·6	1·9	48
Seraya, White	*Parashorea malaanonan*	L	9·9	7·5	191	61·6	3·5	89
		T	9·7	3·5	89	62·0	0·7	18
Sterculia, Brown	*Sterculia rhinopetala*	L	11·0	5·0	127	35·2	2·2	56
		T	10·6	2·3	58	27·4	0·9	23
Sterculia, Yellow	*Sterculia oblonga*	L	10·8	8·3	211	38·7	2·5	64
		T	10·2	2·4	61	37·8	0·7	18
Sycamore	*Acer pseudoplatanus*	L	10·0	6·0	152	—	—	—
		T	—	—	—	—	—	—

*L — Longitudinal with the Face Grain parallel to the length of the specimen.
 T — Transverse with the Face Grain perpendicular to the length of the specimen.
†The radius at which breakages should not exceed 5%.
‡Material of 4 mm thickness.